Lessons from
Mama

This book is about the people who Live in this house,

Joan Walker Page

ISBN 978-1-63874-235-7 (paperback)
ISBN 978-1-63961-999-3 (hardcover)
ISBN 978-1-63874-236-4 (digital)

Christian Faith Publishing, Inc.
832 Park Avenue
Meadville, PA 16335
www.christianfaithpublishing.com

Cover artwork created by author, Joan Walker Page, age 6.

Family Tree Addendum:
Addison Page b. 9-5-2021;
Wells Andrews b. 9-8-2021

Printed in the United States of America

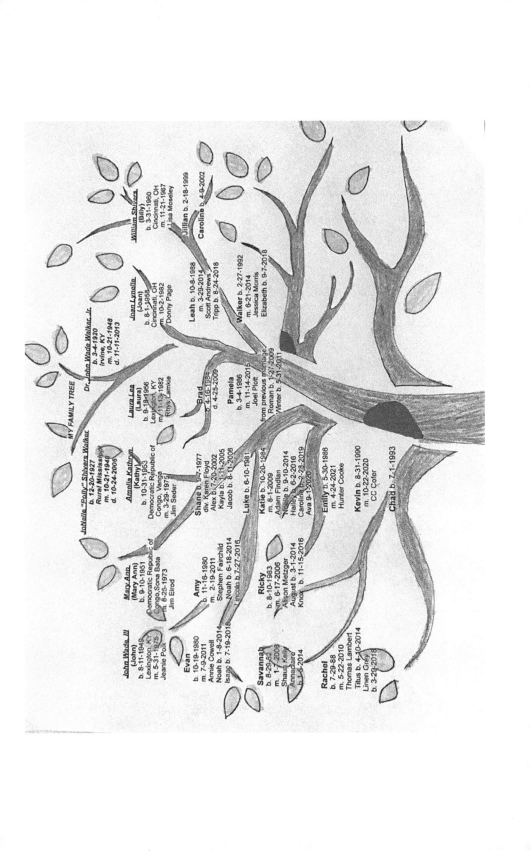

MY FAMILY TREE

The Walker Children, 1962

Billy, Lisa, Jeanie, baby Rachael, John Wade, Mom and Dad, 1988.

I dedicate this work to my two bookend brothers, John Wade and Billy. Without our brothers, these stories would be distinctly different.

I love you, brothers. F.T.

Praises for Lessons From Mama

All of us have lessons from our mothers, but far too few of us ever take time to share those lessons with a broader audience… which is a shame! My friend Joan Page has taken the time to share the all-important lessons that she learned from her mom who lived an incredible life as the wife of a medical missionary. I am also blessed to be Joan and Donny Pages' pastor for the past fifteen years, and I can assure you Joan followed her mother's lessons well in her own personal life.

My mother used to say, "If you don't have something nice to say then say nothing at all." So it gives me pleasure to say plenty about Joan and this wonderful inspirational book, *Lessons from Mama*.

Dr. Dwight "Ike" Reighard
Senior Pastor, Piedmont Church, Marietta, Georgia
CEO, MUST Ministries,
Author of *Treasures of the Dark and
Daily Insights with Zig Ziglar*

I met this energetic, bubbly author, Joan Page, through a mutual friend a few years ago. I am beyond excited and honored she asked me to review her new book, *Lessons from Mama*. I didn't have the privilege of meeting Mama Polly, yet I love her and her lessons. Two short days after reading *Lessons from Mama*, I found myself sharing "Lesson 3: Are You Down? Help Someone!" with a nurse at Emory Hospital in Atlanta. The sweet sentiments flowing from this book are written from a heart filled with love. I connected deeply with

Lessons from Mama, and I daresay I will refer to these lessons for years to come. The lessons are impactful, wise, and evergreen. Thank you, Joan, for sharing your precious mama!

Tammy Stafford
Blogger and author of
Labeled by Humanity, Loved by God

Lessons from Mama transcends age, gender, and race. Whether you are a boy, girl, man, woman, young, old, Black, White, Asian, Hispanic, or another race, this compilation of wise lessons passed down to her children by Polly Shivers Walker has a lesson for you. It chronicles a lifetime of service to her Lord and Savior and others.

It is one thing to learn a lesson. It quite an impactful difference to see a lesson lived. It is true many of us learn what we see lived. Polly Shivers Walkers lives on as her lessons are lived out to this day by her children.

Edward Miller, author of
*Making Sense of Your Money: Solving
The Riddle of Managing Your Money*

Stories are woven into the intricate tapestry of family life. *Lessons from Mama* by Joan Walker Page shares the legacy of matriarch Mama Walker through stories of faith and fortitude that embody the Walker family. Grab a cup of tea and listen in as Joan encourages your heart through the lessons she learned from her dear mother. Each chapter highlights the wisdom Mama Walker imparted to her family. Enjoy homespun lessons universal to us all, enduring truths about love, loyalty, commitment, and perseverance. *Lessons from Mama* will encourage you to love deeper, smile brighter, and pray harder.

Co-Founders of FlourishWriters and FlourishGathering,
Jenny Kochert and Mindy Kiker

Lessons from my Mama is beautifully written with such great detail that I almost felt like I was right there sitting with the author. I first met Joan Walker page as my teacher at Avondale Elementary School. "Miss Walker, " at the time, was a first-year teacher. I remember thinking that she was like a dream and asking myself, How did she get to be so wonderful? Well, now I know. Her mother. The way this author describes her mama is how I saw my fifth-grade teacher so many, many years ago.

Tracey Lindsey Harris, Educator and Childcare Provider

Contents

It is in the middle that human choices are made; the beginning and the end remain with God. The decrees of God are birth and death, and in between those limits man makes his own distress or joy.

—Oswald Chambers

Introduction

I've often wondered how I squeezed into this family. This loving, crazy, godly family, often called The Walker Clan. My folks were married nine years by the time I came along in 1958. Already the pleased, proud parents of four children. First, however, I must give you some important, emerging events that surfaced in the decade before my birth.

My brother, John Wade meets new friends in Sona Bota, 1951.

The year was 1949 and the young new parents, Polly and John Walker, were sailing far away to a distant land to be medical missionaries. Accompanying them was their firstborn baby. A son named John Wade Walker III, nine months old, was in tow. Within the next few years, two daughters, Mary Ann, then Kathy would soon join their big brother, John. His first two little sisters have always enjoyed telling others that their birthplace was the heart of Africa, at that time known as Belgian Congo. After five years in Africa, and now stateside, another little girl, Laura Lea was born in Kentucky, to add to the clan in 1956.

Child number 5, a babe in arms. Me! Easter 1959.

I was always told that they wanted one more son to even the playing field. Accordingly, they kept trying for more. I came next, followed by a second son, William Shivers Walker. Billy. It is honestly unfathomable to imagine life without my little brother. The ideal playmate, Billy brought adventure, laughter, mischief, and smiles to our already rambunctious family life. Six children. An even six.

Daddy as an only child, and Mama, one of four, could not have imagined all of the experiences, the unexpected capers, that lay ahead of them. Escapades that were usual ingredients in oversized families.

On the heels of Billy's birth in 1960, my grandmother, Anna Mae Walker, soon quipped, "Johnny, what are you going to do with all these children?"

It's been said many times that a child has little to no appreciation for how hard it is to be a good parent until they become one. Like most children, I definitely did not understand how challenging parenting was. I did, however, discover early in my life how special my Mama was. I wonder how this truth become apparent to me at a young age? While Daddy worked long hours as a solo physician, Mama was nurturing all of us and still helping a whole slew of other people who showed up in her daily path. While others were away, whether it was to Vietnam or to college in another state, Mama consistently wrote letters to her flock. Mama smiled and laughed. All the time. Mama prayed aloud with all of us and silently, on her own. Mama was down-to-earth, relatable. Mama was optimistic, courageous, a wise woman. Mama loved books. Many of her greatest adventures took place in the stories she would read.

Now, a mom to two married young adults, and a grandmother, "Jojo" to two growing tots and two littles growing in the womb, I have come to realize the benefit of the lessons my Mama taught me. While the number of the lessons is innumerable, I have featured twelve here for my portrayal of our beloved, late Mama.

Over a decade ago, as I began to consider these life lessons, I started my "Pages from Joan" at www.joanwpage.com blog based on them. Overtime, I asked my brothers and sisters to share their ideas about some of the lessons they learned while growing up in our home. We have all agreed that we were blessed with a wise mother and a compassionate, loving father with a strong constitution.

The lessons you will read here were shared with me by my siblings. I then joined their stories with my own memories of lessons learned, as well as my life application of my Mama's lessons. It is my hope that this short book will inspire and encourage both men and women from all walks of life.

We all have this in common: We all have a mother!

Life is a journey. Stories are windows into our souls.

Did you know? Like my mother, we can all leave a positive legacy after we take our last earthly breath.

You and I can absorb lessons from another's stories that will then enhance our life journey?

Let us begin.

Someone is sitting in the shade today because
someone planted a tree a long time ago.

—Warren Buffett

But if I've learned anything about the world of grace,
it's that failure is always a chance for a do-over.

—Brennan Manning

Tell me, what is it you plan to do with
your one wild and precious life?

—Mary Oliver

Lesson 1

Bloom Where You're Planted

This is actually a hard lesson to start with, but it is an important one. It is a lesson that Mama truly lived out loud for the forty-eight years I lived in this world with her. Adopted at age three, Polly Shivers Walker would have never believed the joy-filled life God had in store for her. Perhaps being orphaned at such a young age trained Mama to be extra aware of her circumstances as she made it her aim to grow despite adversity. Since I was born into an established, busy household, I could only imagine what it might be like to be orphaned as a toddler. When referring to her adoption, she always emphasized her gratitude. Gratitude was her way of life, long before society began encouraging folks to be more grateful in order to gain contentment.

It was the summer of 1961. A year and a half had passed since the birth of my little brother, Billy, on March 31, 1960. Daddy had just completed his specialized training to be an obstetrician gynecologist. However, they had not yet determined where he would practice. Where they would plant their family's roots. Sadly, both of my grandfathers had recently passed on within six months of each other. It was time to take the long road trip from northern Kentucky to the suburbs of Atlanta, Georgia. There were eight traveling in our wood-trimmed station wagon. There were no seatbelt laws and, of course, no air-conditioning in the wagon. Sweaty, with the windows wide open, maybe we sang "She'll be comin' 'round the mountain

21

when she comes!" alternating with traveling car games, like finding and tallying a list of license tags. I was only age three, so best I can remember, we just piled in wherever we could find a spot. Maybe there was an assortment of suitcases tied on the top rack with heavy rope. My little brother, Billy, along with Laura, and I were likely on the flat surface in the way back dodging the random cargo and snacks. A mom, a dad, six kids ages twelve down to age eighteen months, one grandmother. Daddy's mother, Mamaw. Oh, and one pet. A parakeet named Pixie. Rumor has it that Pixie nearly died from dehydration on the long journey. I am quite sure there were numerous rest room breaks along the way. State-line rest areas where we could run and play.

With no home and no certain plans on where Daddy would start his private practice in obstetrics, I am now confident that the uncertain future of our family must have weighed heavily on my parents' shoulders. We finally landed at Ponce de Leon Manor Hotel, right on Ponce de Leon Road in Atlanta, Georgia. We spilled out of the wagon, one by one. Even with all of the tremendous lack of certainty, I envision my parents overwhelmingly relieved to arrive. A temporary residence was undoubtedly greater than the cramped, ear-splitting vehicle.

Many years later, Daddy would give an account of his personal, poignant remembrance of those three weeks with us. As his six young children slept soundly, our daddy paced Peachtree Street, praying for God's guidance. I wonder if this was a time when God grew his faith exponentially? An only child, Daddy was raised on The Good Book. He knew that life could be unpredictable. That adversity could grow us as we trusted in God. As he strolled Atlanta streets in the dark of night, passing strangers along the way, he likely mulled scriptures over in his mind. Scriptures like Psalm 46:10, Joshua 1:6, and 1 Corinthians 3:16.

Meanwhile, Mom carried on for more than three weeks in this Atlanta hotel. Like Daddy, she knew God would provide for them as they did their part. Without a doubt, she was thankful that we were able to get most of our meals as Mama cared for us all. Night after night of uncertainty, Mama persevered, she bloomed where she was planted. Before too long, our parents found the perfect home at 655 Webster Drive, in Decatur, Georgia. This would become our family's home for the next three decades. Daddy soon began his practice on Medlock Road, just down the road from what was then DeKalb General Hospital. Here, he would soon gain privileges to deliver babies for a multitude of local Decatur families, always offering complimentary care to families belonging to Ministers of the Gospel.

There were oodles of other instances of this lesson from my Mama, but perhaps the greatest of all happened four and a half decades following our move to Georgia. Mama was told she had a diagnosis of esophageal cancer in July 2006. With grace, strength, and godly confidence, her initial response was, "Well, we're supposed to bloom where we are planted, aren't we?" Heartbreakingly, her disease took her from us a short four months later.

Doesn't everyone hope to leave a legacy behind as they pass on from this earth? I am not sure if Mama thought about this or not.

Either way, Mama managed to leave a strong footprint for her many friends and family members to fall right into. I know that because of her legacy, I find myself thinking about her every day as I journey through the years.

What kind of legacy do you and I want to leave when it is our time to take our leave from this earthly life?

Read on to discover her legacy…the many lessons Mama left behind.

From Mama's Journal

January 3, 1950

Rain-creek rising-John Wade, laughing and playing. We went to Kentucky to visit family. The roads were terrible, but baby John Wade did not mind at all. I think he likes adventures, too, just like us.

From Joan's Journal

Friday, February 16, 1996

I am feeling a real growth in my spirit after meeting my new friend, Joyce Truitt here on the Big Island of Hawaii during our conference vacation. Joyce lives in Turlock, California, and has been married to her husband, Ralph, for 52 years, compared to our nearly 14 years of marriage. How inspiring! Joyce has given me tips on parenting and a strong medical marriage. I am thankful for our new friendship.

Wednesday, June 28, 2006

Amazing how so much can change in just a few short hours. Mama's GI MD, Dr. Kommor, just let us all know that Mama has cancerous cells in her esophagus and lymph nodes. When Mama heard the news, she stated bravely, "Well, we are supposed to bloom where we are planted, and I am too blessed to be stressed." She is a rock! More to come...

Thursday, September 21, 2006

I received another letter today from my friend, Joyce Truitt. Her note told me that as she was "down-sizing", she was hoping to "Bloom Where She Was Planted." The exact words my Mama used on 6/28/06, when she first heard of her cancer diagnosis, and Joyce does not even know about Mama's illness!!! Joyce also sent me a blessing magnet with this same mantra. There are no coincidences in our relationship with God,

only divine appointments. I believe God used
Joyce to encourage me today with her note.

I have always enjoyed writing things down since I was a small girl. Watching Mama as she bloomed wherever she was planted has prompted me to be sensitive to others who are called to the same response. I realize that distressing life events happen to everyone. Some, definitely more harrowing than others.

The day was Sunday, March 8, 2015, early in the morning. Donny and I were sleeping in, knowing we would rise soon enough to head to church. The phone ringing drew me out of bed and the voice on the other end was a friend I had met in Southwest Virginia through our lifelong friends, Kelly and Paul Read. "Have you heard about The Reads?" Dianne asked me anxiously.

"No," I answered quickly, bracing myself for what would come next. "Taylor has passed suddenly!" Taylor, nearly age twenty-four, was the second child of The Reads, and one we had loved since he was in utero. As I screamed out with tears, Donny jumped out of bed to begin to digest the same devastating news. Taylor was gone.

While we have not lost a child, Donny and I have faced the passing of all of our birth parents. We have also gone through the homegoing of some precious friends and other family members. We all experience grief in one way or another as we journey through this thing called life. Grief is certain in each one of our lives.

Since we have been closely connected to The Reads for decades beforehand, as well as during this season of grief, I have some reflections I feel compelled to share here.

> "Tell me, what is it you plan to do with your one wild and precious life?"
>
> Mary Oliver

Taylor Read, two years old, 1993.

"Example is not the main thing in influencing others. It's the only thing."

Dr. Albert Schweitzer, German theologian, organist, philosopher, physician, and medical missionary to Africa, 1875–1964

Moving forward, this family has intentionally focused on faith, family, and friends. They have purposefully played outdoors any chance they get, whether it is walking their four-legged companion, Player, biking on the Virginia Creeper Trail, or tilling and planting in Mom's garden behind their Abingdon, Virginia home. Kelly, Paul, and Megan Read have bloomed where they've been planted.

Marrying just forty-eight days before us, in 1982, The Reads have maintained a strong marriage partnership. They have taken in good music to soothe their soul, and enjoyed yummy food from their Big Green Egg. They have made sure to welcome continual fellowship with family and friends. The Reads have stayed connected to their church family, which nourishes each other during times of need. This decision was clear after Taylor's passing when "Lift High The Cross," this song was chosen to be played as the family was ushered out following his Celebration of Life service.

The Reads have enjoyed many performances, whether at The Barter Theater or the incredible shows at The Biltmore Concert Series in Asheville, North Carolina.

Along with the help of friends, family, the caring community of Abingdon, Virginia, accompanied by the Virginia Creeper Trail Club, this family has brought about a unique "shelter from the storm" alongside The Holston River. This safe haven was dedicated in October 2015. Designed by Taylor's accomplished and artistic sister, Megan Read, this is a picturesque spot all should visit at some point in the future. Because of Taylor's tremendous love for all things outdoors, the shelter is a perfect site to reflect on the preciousness of life and the legacy of Taylor Heston Read.

Already, this shelter has brought rest to many. Bikers and kay-akers have sought refuge here. Taylor's Shelter has even been a venue for a few weddings.

Yes, Taylor Read loved all things outdoors. Golfing, hunting, boating, or biking on the well-known Virginia Creeper Trail. It is dif-ficult to imagine a more fitting, more suitable choice for this unique sanctuary.

I have a couple of questions for you and for me today. How will we respond in our time of grief and hardship? Will we follow the example of this courageous family, looking up with hope in the future? Will you and I bloom where we are planted?

I hope you will. I hope I will too.

When is the last time you meandered through your garden on a sunny early evening with a glass of wine, or on a chilly spring morn-ing with a steaming mug of coffee?

Perhaps you do not have a garden where you live. In that case, consider taking advantage of a local garden in your community: Gibbs Gardens, Atlanta Botanical Gardens, Barnsley Gardens, and Smith-Gilbert Gardens are just a few we can find near our Marietta, Georgia, home.

We can learn so much from hanging out in a garden, whether we yield beautiful flowering plants, fruits, or vegetables.

Walking quietly, slowly through a garden area will remind us that life is all about change. Change can happen quickly or slowly. Life can be downright scary at times. We can look to our faith and nature to help replenish our courage.

> "To plant a garden is to believe in tomorrow."
>
> Audrey Hepburn

The buds on a branch compared with a full bloom on the same branch echoes the truth that progress is impossible without change.

Did you know? There is a longtime legend about the dogwood tree. It is called The Legend of the Dogwood Tree. The dogwood goes through dramatic changes throughout a year's time...first white, then pale pink, before the leaves turn a crimson red in autumn.

One of my Mama's favorite parts of spring were the many bright purple wisteria vines skirting the roads and highways. I had to stop and take some pictures of this down the street from us, right outside the entrance of Signal Hill Subdivision. As I walked up to it and took in its sweet fragrance, childhood memories came flooding back...of wisteria, the circular azalea garden in our front yard, and countless dandelions that we laughingly blew into each other's faces.

Although my friends Brenda, Kelly, and Ellen are amazing gardeners, I am not very good at gardening. I forget to water my pots and the plants don't like that very much, lol.

Though my sis, Laura Lea, and I were raised under the same roof, I did not receive the same green thumb she now has as her indoor plants are varied and numerous. I started my very first herb garden in 2013, and then changes happened with my Daddy's passing on November 11 of that same year. With two weddings in 2014 within eleven weeks of each other, my interest in an herb garden waned and remained dry through 2015 as we cared for Donny's dad. This spring, I am determined to revive my herb garden and have gotten started with a few purchases of basil, sage, and dill. Now if I can just be sure my herbs get plenty of water during what is sure to be another hot summer in Georgia!

Now before we move onto the next lesson Mama taught me, let's look at five thoughts we can apply to our lives while hanging out in a garden. A place we can work on blooming where we are planted.

1. Some things just can't be rushed. They are worth the wait. Have patience.
2. You have to be willing to do the dirty, hard jobs (weeding, digging, spreading manure) in order to yield the wonderful results.

Paul Read working in his Abingdon, Virginia garden.

3. A garden reminds us to make plans, to have vision, and grow big dreams.
4. A garden reminds us to be grateful, to have daily gratitude for nature and for life which are miracles. And they are free!

5. It is hard to garden alone, and it is impossible to do life alone as well. It takes community to thrive!

A garden is both a healer and a teacher.
What are some other lessons you and I can learn from a garden?

A Related Blog Post

April 8, 2020

6 Ways We Can Relieve Stress
How To Bloom Where We Are Planted During A Pandemic
An Acronym

Do you have a lot of stress in your life these days? With all of the changing news of the pandemic, day-by-day, it would be no surprise to anyone that our stress levels are at an all-time high.

We are all getting a taste of a slower lifestyle, one that came unannounced, unplanned, and topped with an uncertain future.

What has slowing down meant for you? Have you and I stopped to think about our days gone by when we were so busy that we could barely catch our breath? I think it is a good opportunity to look at that busy life and see what changes might be possible going forward.

Today, I will share with you six ways we can begin to relieve our stress starting today.

S-Seize the moment, pause and be IN the moment. Realize that these few minutes may be all we have. Breathe deeply connecting with your heart.

T-Take a break to meditate and pray… whatever that means for you. Express gratitude.

While you are taking a break, consider coloring, collaging, escaping for a bubble bath, or taking a walk alone. Exaggerated self-care is vital during this time of sheltering in. As a Christ-follower, I have learned that He meets me right where I am whenever I reach out to Him. I'm so thankful for this truth.

R-Rest enough. I know this is easier said than done. Especially for parents and teachers who are currently homeschooling when they were not used to doing it. Insufficient sleep puts us on edge. Try setting the timer on your phone and stretch out for a 15-25 minute power nap. At night, keep your screens away from your bedside table. It is particularly important to do this before sleep as it can cut down many of the problems related to insomnia and other sleep disorders.

E-Be sure to get some exercise, even if it is a simple walk around your workplace parking lot during your lunch break. Move. Stretch. Stretch. Move. Exercise will pump up your endorphins, improving your mood.

S-As many have been sharing on social media, this is actually a perfect time to declutter your spaces. I have found that an uncluttered space = less stress. Watch YouTube videos for ideas and the motivation to get started. Shed Stuff. Even after the Pandemic, keep a "give away" box handy and put things in there on a regular basis. Most will agree that we just have too much stuff! Let's give things away that are still useful and unclutter our lives some to help us relieve stress.

S-Screen Time Reduced. Most of us, if we were completely honest, spend way too much time looking at screens during our waking hours.

The preoccupation with our devices, even during free time can often mess up other schedules causing delays in routine work, creating unwanted stress. Regulating screen time can help individuals block out at least some of the channels through which stress is stimulated. During this extra time at home, consider creating a "cell phone basket" where all phones can take a break from their humans. This is especially important during mealtime and family board game time.

Which of these six ideas will you and I incorporate into our lives in the days ahead?

As we continue to heal from a global pandemic, we will grow and grow. We will bloom where we are planted, though it can be an arduous task!

Therefore, we need to make time to carve out plenty of opportunities for fun. Mama inevitably did! And as she always said,

"We can sleep when we're dead!

"Then I realized that to be more alive, I had to be less afraid.
So I did it. I lost my fear and gained my whole life."

Anonymous

"Reflect upon your present blessings—-of
which every man has many—-not on your past
misfortunes, of which all men have some."

Charles Dickens

"The world is big and I want to have a good
look at it before it gets dark."

John Muir

Lesson 2

You Can Sleep When You're Dead

M ama loved an adventure! She was always in line to experience something novel and fun, no matter what time of day it took place. Many times, these capers involved sleep deprivation, at which Mama would declare, "You can sleep when you're dead!"

These adventures rarely involved much money. Mom always emphasized the simple things in life. Mama loved the arts; musicals like *Fiddler on the Roof* and *The Sound of Music* brought her much delight.

Mama did most of her traveling in the thousands of books she would read during her lifetime. She did, however, jump at the chance to travel to Germany three times for the famous play, *The Passion Play*. Mama's three times came about in 1950 with Daddy, in 1984 with a girlfriend, Mary Lou Shults, and in 1990 with a few others and me.

The play enacts the life of Jesus, covering the short final period of his life from his visit to Jerusalem and leading to his execution by crucifixion. *The Passion Play* is performed by the inhabitants of the small, old-world village of Oberammergau. The intriguing back story on why this small village has continued to perform this play every decade is astounding! The historical account surrounds an outbreak of a bubonic plague which devastated Bavaria during The Thirty Years' War (1618–1648). The village of Oberammergau remained plague-free until September 25, 1633. Soon, over the next thirty-three days, eighty-one villagers would die, half of Oberammergau's population. On October 28, 1633, the villagers vowed that if God spared them from the plague, they would perform a play every ten years depicting the life and death of Jesus. Even though this horrific plague had raged in many parts of Europe, including Oberammergau, nobody died of plague in Oberammergau after that vow. The villagers kept their word to God by performing *The Passion Play* for the first time in 1634, and every ten years following.

Along with my sis, Mary Ann, her husband, Jim, my Daddy and my husband, Donny, we had the unique opportunity to join Mama for her third visit, the 1990 performance of *The Passion Play*. We stayed in hospitable host homes in this small German village, and all enjoyed an unforgettable experience of a lifetime. This trip was quite an adventure in itself! Thankfully, my sister, Laura Lea and her husband, Rhys looked after our two-year-old Leah back home.

Our 1990 Oberammergau tour group.

Sadly, the every-decade, 2020 *Passion Play* was postponed to the year of 2022 due to the global COVID-19 Pandemic. The 2020 play was sold out as the village expected 450,000 guests from around the globe. The good news is that tickets for 2022 went on sale in

October 2020! The participants in the play are required to have been born in Oberammergau or a resident for a minimum of twenty years. Nearly two thousand residents have applied to be involved in the 2022 presentation, the Forty-Second *Passion Play*. A production that is five hours in length, beginning at 2:30 p.m. and ending at 10:30 p.m. There is a three-hour intermission for dinner. It is anticipated that over 750,000 will travel to Oberammergau, Germany, in 2022. *The Passion Play* theater is open, with a magnificent, mountainous background. I dream of returning for my second visit in honor and in memory of my Mama's adventurous spirit.

One of my favorite memories involved what often happened after dinner at home on Webster Drive. The newspaper would be opened wide across the table as we searched excitedly for a movie we could make it to. Once decided, we would rush to our rooms, slipping on shoes, grabbing our purses, run out the front door, and jump in the car. Racing down the street to either Toco Hills or the North DeKalb Mall Cinema, we would arrive right on time, or just a minute or two late.

Either way, there was always time for a quick stop at the concession stand for popcorn and an ice-cold Coca-Cola.

One particular night, we arrived after the theater was very dark, so we followed Mama closely in a line. Mom led us down a row and inadvertently sat in a man's lap. As he called out in surprise, our clan threw it in reverse, backing out of the row as fast as we could, snickering as we went!

Another time, in her haste, to make it on time to a movie, Mama put on two different shoes—a black one and a navy one. One shoe was flat, while the other one had a small heel. Well, actually Mama never admitted to the different sized heels, always saying, "They were different colors, but they were the same heel!" We howled over these memories for decades, and we still get tickled as we recall them today.

Mama taught us and many of our friends how to play the card game, Canasta, a favorite pastime in the Rummy game family. Players attempt to make melds of seven cards of the same rank and "go out" by playing all cards in their hand. We would set up two, or even three-tables in the den and play for hours. Anytime Mama was dealt a deuce, it was time to freeze the deck! As the night of play continued, Mom would beg for, "one more round," even playing after 1:00 a.m. on countless nights. To this day, my husband and I love dealing out the playing cards to our kids and their spouses after the tots are tucked safely in bed. Though, our son-in-law, Scott never had the chance to meet my Mama, he follows in her steps by freezing the deck any chance he gets.

As this goes to print, taking account of the many married spouses, there are twenty-seven grandchildren and twenty great-grandchildren that have come from the six Walker Clan kids and their spouses! Though that number seems to change often with marriage plans in the works and babies on the way.

Many of these grandchildren live by the lessons you will read about in this book. An example of this involves our niece, Amy Elrod Fairchild in 2003. Amy was living with her Brazilian family while studying Portuguese in preparation to become a medical missionary in Rio de Janeiro, Brazil. At one point when everyone was worn out from some adventure, Amy stated in English, "Oh well, like my GoodMama always says, we can sleep when we're dead!" Her Brazilian mother asked her to translate the phrase and Amy found this to be very difficult because of the differences in the languages. They shared lots of laughs over this lesson and her Brazilian mother habitually used this statement many times afterward.

> "Dance as if no one is watching, sing as if no one were listening, and live every day as if it were your last."
>
> Irish proverb

Please understand that Mama did make sure to rest. In fact, after a huge, weekly Sunday Southern lunch of pot roast, sweet, iced tea, sides of lima beans, buttery mashed potatoes, creamed corn, pear halves with mayo and grated cheese, followed by a delicious pound cake or a banana pudding, Mama would excuse herself from the table. There was an unspoken understanding that the kids—usually the four girls—would ensure that all the food was put away and the kitchen was cleaned up.

Mama would spend a minimum of three hours resting. As the years clicked by and grands were added to our family, this naptime became a tradition. Known by the visiting grandchildren as GoodMama's "afternoon siesta," they knew they were required to have one too. No matter their age, toddler, teen and in between. It was expected that all in the home would rest through the afternoon when at GoodMama and GoodDaddy's house. Also expected was a bundle of grandparenting fun upon waking.

As parents and grandparents, what are some activities we can incorporate into our time with the littles in our lives…unforgettable pursuits or pastimes?

I was reminded of Mama's adventurous spirit recently when I read about a letter from a vibrant young lady by the name of Holly Butcher. Holly's post has gone viral and is full of inspiration on how to make the moments count.

We may know a bit about this horrific disease that took Holly from this earth in 2018. Sadly, our Piedmont Church friends, Dixie and Benny Buice lost their precious daughter, Christy at age twenty-one to this same illness, Ewing Sarcoma.

Christy loved kids and had plans to become an elementary teacher. Kindergarten. We all have dreams, don't we!? Christy graduated from Lassiter High School and went onto Kennesaw State University near her home. KSU was so good to her, as she went through her treatments at Scottish Rite every four weeks or so, missing classes often. They let her continue and Christy worked hard to keep up. Christy volunteered at Camp Sunshine. She went the first time as a camper, the second time as a trainee, and the third time she was not able to continue. Christy loved being there, just working with the kids. The counselors loved her so much. Christy was a reliable babysitter, however passed her jobs onto her best friend, Michelle, when she realized she should not keep the kids alone. She was not ready to quit sitting, but she knew it was the right decision. Christy loved writing letters to her parents and close friends near the end of her earthly life. These letters were both "thank you notes" and "friendship notes."

The Buice Family remembers their Christy, with thankfulness and pride for the time they had with her on this earth.

Christy Buice (January 18, 1978–October 20, 1999) is pictured here with her favorite pup, Precious.

There are many verses in the Bible about the brevity of our earthly life.

Read here what Australian Holly Butcher wanted to relay to whomever would listen before she took her leave in the new year of 2018:

Butcher's poignant post is definitely worth reading in full. But here are 16 especially powerful points:

1. "I just want people to stop worrying so much about the small, meaningless stresses in life and try to remember that we all have the same fate after it all, so do what you can to make your time feel worthy and great, minus the bullshit… Those times you are [whining] about ridiculous things (something I have noticed so much these past few months), just think about someone who is really facing a problem. Be grateful for your minor issue and get over it. It's OK to acknowledge that something is annoying but try not to carry on about it and negatively affect other people's days."

2. "Once you do that, get out there and take a freaking big breath of that fresh Aussie air deep in your lungs, look at how blue the sky is and how green the trees are; It is so beautiful. Think how lucky you are to be able to do just that—breathe. You might have got caught in bad traffic today or had a bad sleep because your beautiful babies kept you awake, or your hairdresser cut your hair too short… I swear you will not be thinking of those things when it is your turn to go. It is all SO insignificant when you look at life as a whole. I'm watching my body waste away right before my eyes with nothing I can do about it and all I wish for now is that I could have just one more birthday or Christmas with my family, or just one more day with my partner and dog. Just one more."

3. "I hear people complaining about how terrible work is or about how hard it is to exercise—be grateful you are physically able to. Work and exercise may seem like such trivial things…until your body doesn't allow you to do either of them. Appreciate your good health and functioning body—even if it isn't your ideal size. Look after it and embrace how amazing it is."

4. "Give, give, give. It is true that you gain more happiness doing things for others than doing them for yourself. I wish I did this more. Since I have been sick, I have met the most incredibly giving and kind people and been the receiver of the most thoughtful and loving words and support from my family, friends and strangers; more than I could ever give in return. I will never forget this and will be forever grateful to all of these people."

5. "This year, our family agreed to do no presents and despite the tree looking rather sad and empty (I nearly cracked Christmas Eve!), it was so nice because people didn't have the pressure of shopping and the effort went into writing a nice card for each other. Plus, imagine my family trying to buy me a present knowing they would probably end up with it themselves…strange!…but those cards mean more to me than any impulse purchase could… Anyway, moral of the story—presents are not needed for a meaningful Christmas."

6. "Use your money on experiences…or at least don't miss out on experiences because you spent all your money on material shit. Put in the effort to do that day trip to the beach you keep putting off. Dip your feet in the water and dig your toes in the sand. Wet your face with salt water."

7. "Try just enjoying and being in moments rather than capturing them through the screen of your phone. Life isn't meant to be lived through a screen nor is it about getting the perfect photo."

A Colorado visit with our Sam Hill Gang! March 2017. Gatherings with friends and family add so much to our days.

8. "Listen to music…really listen. Music is therapy."

9. "Cuddle your dog. Far out, I will miss that."

Molly West's dog, Ranger meets our new pup, Camden Court "Cami" Page.

10. "Talk to your friends. Put down your phone. Are they doing OK?"
11. "Travel if it's your desire, don't if it's not."
12. "Work to live, don't live to work."
13. "Seriously, do what makes your heart feel happy."

ART matters, and it sure makes me happy! Here I am with dk Gallery artist, Holly Irwin and my original piece by Holly: Country Meadow. The girl in the piece is "me" when I was my younger self. (www.dkgallery.us)

14. "Don't feel pressured to do what other people might think is a fulfilling life. You might want a quieter life and that is so OK."
15. "Tell your loved ones you love them every time you get the chance and love them with everything you have."

16. "Oh and one last thing. If you can, do a good deed for humanity, start regularly donating blood. It will make you feel good with the added bonus of saving lives. Blood donation (more bags than I could keep up with counting) helped keep me alive for an extra year—a year I will be forever grateful that I got to spend here on Earth with my family, friends and dog. A year I had some of the greatest times of my life."

Wow, just wow!

A Related Blog Post

June 13, 2016

Climb Every Mountain
Do you have dreams for the future?

Have you begun to let some of those dreams slip away? Nearly one year ago, my hiking buddy, Kathy invited me to join her and three girlfriends for a hiking adventure. I immediately said yes, not knowing that this past week, our eight-hour hike up, viewing the sunset from a 7,000-foot vista, and trekking back down in six hours would inspire me so. After my recent climb up to the Summit of Mt. Le Conte in the Great Smoky Mountains, my dreams have been rekindled. Laughing, singing Rod Stewart, songs from musicals, Carole King, and JT, telling long stories, and "unplugging for a time" all served to rejuvenate and inspire the five of us!

It has been said that "getting old is not for sissies," and as I am now living in my sixth decade,

I am finding this to be true. Life, at any stage, takes great courage. Climbing a huge mountain has helped to decrease my fears and rebuild my courage for the days ahead.

I was able to celebrate my friend, Cyndi's 60th surprise birthday party this past Saturday. A friend I saw there shared that she found it hard to do things for herself during this season of her life, with grown married children and grandchildren now here. I told her about the 3 nights I snuck away to Tennessee to climb Mt. Le Conte with friends, and how doing that (I am hoping) will make me a stronger and more loving woman, Mother, and Mom-In-Law, as well as a Grandma to our (future) grandchildren. <smile>

So, what are the dreams you have had in your past that might be trying to slip away because of time and circumstances? What's on your list, what "mountains" would you like to climb to gain serenity and hope for the future? Our adventure happened to be extremely physically challenging, but your dreams and my dreams can be whatever they are, unique to each one of us: keeping a journal, visiting a historical nearby community you've been thinking of, increasing your fitness, snagging 15-30 minutes each day for some solitude, some alone time, and more. Take a few moments to sit quietly, perhaps with pen and paper at hand, and jot down a few of your dreams.

Dreams CAN come true, like the rigorous hike that five women, including a social worker, three nurses, and a teacher, all in our fifties took on June 7-8, 2016. Though there are no showers or electricity at the top, the Mt. Le Conte staff took great care of us feeding us delicious, family style meals.

Getting started at Newfound Gap. The first 2.7 miles of Boulevard Trail is part of the AT!

Let's Keep Our Dreams Alive!

From Mama's Journal

May 1, 1982

'It is difficult to steer a parked car, so get moving.'
Henrietta Mears

We are entering a busy summer. Jeanie and Jim S. are living here. (Jim is teaching and Jeanie, with two-year-old, Evan is expecting late-summer) The girls, Joan and Laura are planning weddings, six weeks apart this Fall. Grateful for the space and resources to take care of everything these days. Guess we will sleep when we are dead.

From Joan's Journal

Monday, July 30, 2012

I'm in the backseat of JE's car with Janny co-piloting. The three of us are headed to Knoxville, Tennessee to hook up with Susan, Jo Ann, Leslie and Delo for an overnight adventure! We're staying at The Swift river house, and tubing down the river!

I'm so tired…mostly emotionally. But as Mama always said, "You can sleep when you're dead." So, I will keep going, and rest here in the car along the way. Thankfully, I brought my pillow!

So while Mama was leading the pack in the adventure department, the years flew by. Our family had sweet seasons and we had stretches that took our smiles away for a time. During those times we dealt with sadness, Mama encouraged us to help someone. This tactic impacted us greatly. By helping another, we in turn bolstered ourselves up.

"The purpose of life is not to be happy. It is to be useful, to be honorable, to be compassionate, to have it make some difference that you have lived and lived well."

Ralph Waldo Emerson

"Sometimes the smallest things take up the most room in our hearts."

Winnie the Pooh

"No one has ever become poor by giving."

Anne Frank

"Those who are happiest are those who do the most for others."

Booker T. Washington

Lesson 3

Are You Down? Help Someone!

This is a lesson I've practiced again and again in my life journey. We all have times when we feel discouraged, even hopeless. If we pull up our bootstraps, and help someone, they will be encouraged, and we will feel better too. This works like a charm every time! Try it the next time you feel blue.

It was in early August 2005, when I received the news that my beloved friend, Jil had passed on unexpectedly. Her family was delighting in the final hazy, lazy days of summer when she slipped away. She was forty years old. Jil was one of those humans who inspired others to laugh and love. Jil is still remembered and missed by multitudes of people, even now over fifteen years following her passing. Jil left a memorable legacy behind for her family and friends.

Jil Cain.

My memory bank holds many, many sweet images of this precious friend. One of these was our participation, along with my girlfriend Kathy Owen, in an Avon three-day sixty-mile Breast Cancer Walk together in 2000. With the help of my friend, Jules Furr, I was able to raise over $6,000. I walked in memory of my teaching friend Debbie Ledford who had died in late 1999 of cancer. Our children, Leah and Walker even held a dog-wash to raise funds.

Joan and Jil at the Avon three-day sixty-mile Breast Cancer Walk, 2000.

Throughout this weekend in 2000, Jil, Kathy and I were surrounded by courageous survivors at every turn. All wearing pink. The sixty-mile journey was an incredibly inspiring experience. A stirring of the soul.

An experience that changed our lives forever.

Later in the month of August 2005, soon after my friend had passed, I was driving aimlessly down the road. Our children were at Wednesday night youth group, my husband was working late, and

I was falling into the depths of despondency as I grieved the loss of my forty-year-old girlfriend. Grief like this can rip us open heart and soul and leave us exhausted, gasping for air.

Suddenly, I remembered this important lesson that my mother had always told me. "When you are down, Joan, help someone!"

Mama had often modeled this lesson so well.

Mama knew that some intentional actions in life did not fit neatly into a schedule, especially when it came to giving a hand up to those in her path.

Tragically, Hurricane Katrina and the broken levies had just flooded New Orléans. In the nearby Boots Ward Recreational Center, there was a Red Cross shelter, a safe haven for some of the Katrina evacuees. I drove straight to this center and found out that there was a volunteer position available for the following Monday, 6:00–10:00 a.m. I signed up and felt the sadness start to ease.

A few days later, I arrived at my appointed time, unaware that someone was about to be placed in my path who would change my life forever. I soon met Sarah L. Johnson, a Katrina evacuee who had resided in New Orléans her entire life. Sarah was eighty-five years old, had never married, and had no children. Funny, she said she had always wanted to visit Atlanta, but didn't realize she would come like this. The tale of how she got here is a story in and of itself. After the initial evacuation, though there was a power outage, Sarah and her fellow residents were returned to their apartments. When she heard banging on her door, she glanced out the window only to find that the water was rushing into the streets and rising rapidly. We now know that the levies had broken down, but at that time, the residents had no idea what the rushing water was from. They were hurried to the roof of the building where they stayed overnight until a helicopter could pluck each one of them off the roof. When boarding the helicopter, in all the confusion, this eighty-five-year-old woman lost her walker, her glasses, her shoes, and worst of all Sarah was separated from a friend who was holding all of her IDs for her.

Sometimes our greatest disappointments are God's appointments to be a blessing in someone else's life. A friendship soon developed with eighty-five-year-old Sarah which would change my life.

When I first met Sarah, she was just waking up in the Red Cross Shelter. I helped Sarah with her laundry, got her breakfast. She talked with me about her strong faith in God and how surely God had a plan for her even in this crazy situation. Feeling more encouraged, at the end of my shift, I gave her a hug, thinking I'd never see her again this side of heaven.

Sarah and Joan, 2005.

A few days later, I received a phone call from my friend, Vicki, who had worked at the same shelter, telling me that Sarah needed to see a cardiologist and asking if I could help her to get in to see someone. I had the privilege of taking her to a caring doctor, Dr. Diosdado Irlandez, the very next day. Her heart was just fine, and this was the beginning of a sweet friendship, one that I will forever cherish. After four weeks at the shelter, Sarah moved to a wonderful nearby assisted living facility where even though she was the only evacuee there, she was embraced by the other residents. She worshipped with us at our church and even gathered at my sister, Mary Ann's home for a huge family lunch! She shared her heart with me and told me why Psalm 27 was her mainstay scripture. Mama and I took her to the Martin Luther King Center in Atlanta. She told Mama and me all about her personal, vivid memories of the Civil Rights Movement.

Later, Sarah was happily returned to New Orléans to her same first floor apartment. I believe that our God gave me this opportunity to serve and help Sarah during a time when my heart was shattered over the loss of my cherished friend, Jil.

So if you are feeling down and going through a great disappointment today, look up and all around. Watch for the divine appointment that may be waiting around the corner for you to be an uplifting messenger to someone today.

My older brother, John Wade recalls how Mama was a great listener, who could easily empathize with someone who was troubled. Mama and Dad joined the local organization of "Parents of Marines," providing both comfort and support to those parents whose sons were killed or severely wounded during the Vietnam War, which John Wade fought in. They continued this support long after John was honorably discharged from The Marines to begin college. My sister, Kathy remembers how Mama taught us to look people in the eyes when speaking with them, and always be on the lookout for ways to serve.

I am so thankful to our Mama for teaching this important tool for moving forward when things seem impossibly hard. I use this tool often, and I hope you will too!

This recent year, 2020, has been a discouraging time for so many. And for countless families, the loss of life has been their reality.

Many have asked the question, "How will our children, our teens, our collegiate be impacted by this timeframe in history?"

Dr. Ike Reighard is the senior pastor of our church in Marietta, Georgia, Piedmont Church. Pastor Ike talked about how we can be a good steward of our finances in a message on January 24, 2021. As he shared, he told a story about how a young boy had raised money for the homeless community during the COVID-19 global pandemic. During this story, he reminded us that not all philanthropists are wealthy. A philanthropist can be anyone who has a heart of good will toward others and a desire to help those in his/her path. I pondered this in reference to helping someone when we are going through a difficult patch. Undoubtedly, both the giver and the recipient will be changed when a hand up is offered.

How will you and I respond the next time we feel blue? Discouragement is part of the human experience. However, when we help someone who is struggling in some way, our endorphins and serotonin will increase. We will be encouraged, while another fellow human has been giving a helping hand.

A Related Blog Post

March 18, 2015

Joy Comes in the Morning

"Yes, weeping may endure for the night, but joy does come with the morning."—Psalm 30:5

I've always loved the name "Pamela," since my niece Pamela, born in 1986 has been a special part of my life. So when this young homeless woman told me her name, I just smiled to myself.

The day was a sunny Sunday morning, March 15, 2015. I walked and walked in the beautiful city of San Diego, California, while my husband, Donny, attended a conference. As I moved along, I hummed a favorite song, seeing the lyrics in my mind: Brave, by Sara Bareilles. Carrying my Bible close to my heart, my plans were to find a Presbyterian Church about one mile from our hotel and worship there at the 11:00 service. I soon discovered that instead, my day would be spent in "a church" on the streets of San Diego and not inside the walls of a building. Heavy-hearted, with my husband's dear Dad on my mind with his recent hospitalization in the CCU with pneumonia, paired with grief over the very recent passing of the son of our precious friends the Reads, I sat on a bench to rest right outside The Old Spaghetti Factory, at the corner of 5ᵗʰ and K in the Gaslamp District. Weeping quietly, I took this picture of my Bible, my cup of hot coffee, and a San Diego map.

Just after taking this picture, as I glanced to my right, I saw this woman standing alone right next to my bench. Homelessness is a concern in every big city across our great big world, and sunny San Diego is no exception. In fact, locals this past weekend told us countless times that the reason for their multitude of homeless folks is because of their year-round pleasant climate.

Make it Count: an easy way to make donations
to help the homeless in San Diego.

To help minimize panhandling on every corner, the local San Diego community installed meters like this one to collect pocket change to aid those without a home. I thought this was a good idea to share with folks at MUST Ministries back in Georgia who work tirelessly to help the down and out in our hometown community. Many humans have similar thoughts regarding the homeless population, wondering how they got there, are they alcoholics or addicts, is mental illness a part of their day, and isn't it "their fault" that they are in this situation? Raised by such compassionate parents, my heart has always been tender toward these souls in need. In fact, back in 2002, when Leah was in 8th grade, I taught her class all I knew about this subject, using Phil Collins's Another Day in Paradise as a spring-board. And after recently reading Yankoski's story in the book *Under the Overpass*, my heart has become even softer toward these folks in need, believing "every heartbeat has a story."

"I am like a pencil in God's hand. He does the thinking. He does the writing. The pencil has only to be allowed to be used."

Mother Teresa

So when this woman showed up right next to me, my response was not a surprise to me. And when she shared her name, Pamela, I smiled through my tears, understanding intuitively that her being there was no accident. Pamela is my niece's name, the sister of my late nephew Brad. Though Pam, all alone in this big city, did not approach me, I invited her to have a seat on the bench as I moved myself and my things over. Note: I am not looking for accolades with my story, I simply followed my heart like I do in most every circumstance I find myself in these days. Pam was not the only one who was in need, *I was in need*, as well, and I believe that was the reason she was placed in my path that day.

First things first, I figured she was hungry. She nodded. Waiting for our table at a quaint sidewalk cafe, I was struck by the irony of a pleasant young hostess would soon escort us to our table, quietly folding napkins for the many guests who would be by for a meal on this Sunday.

As we sat across from each other, Pam told me her story. She was stranded in San Diego and needed to get back to Austin, Texas, she had no money to her name, and there was a safe home for her in Texas with her boyfriend and his mother. Though I did not tell her this, and I certainly wasn't sure how the day would play out, I knew by the time we finished our omelets that my husband and I would be her ticket back to Austin.

With a full stomach and a good break in the cafe's clean restaurant bathroom, Pamela and I hit the sidewalk, first purchasing her a big backpack and then heading to nearby Macy's. We went through several different departments, finding her new lingerie, t-shirts, jeans, and socks. Each time we made a purchase, the employee would snip off the tags, and Pam would slip back into the dressing room to change into her new things, coming out with an appreciative, humble smile on her face. Later, when Pastor Ike called me from Georgia, and I burst into tears telling him all about our friends who had lost their son and Donny's Daddy, Pamela was the one who was consoling me, putting her arm around me and whispering how sorry she was for my sadness. I shared with Pastor Ike about who was standing next to me and he said, "Joan, that is exactly what I spoke about in my message this morning."

We packed her backpack full, including her old, used, soiled things which went into a plastic bag until Pam would be able to find a way to wash them. An affordable ticket was purchased at a nearby Greyhound Bus Terminal, and I left Pamela to wait until the 10:45 p.m. departure. Just before 10:30 p.m., Donny and I were strolling around downtown with some friends from Georgia, The Kleinmans and The Reitmans, when I realized we were only a few minutes from the terminal. We said good night to our friends, and walked a few more minutes arriving in time for Donny to meet Pamela and for us to bid her farewell. Pamela's trip would take 36 hours arriving mid-morning on Tuesday, March 17, 2015, and Pamela would call me to let me know she had arrived safely.

Pamela was so appreciative to have her ticket to Austin, Texas.

It was an indisputable fact that my husband and I could not solve the huge problem of homelessness in San Diego, California, but we made a difference for that one beating heart—which at the same time made an even bigger difference for our own hurting hearts.

Our annual TTU gathering, January 2015,
Abingdon, Virginia in The Reads Home.

The Reads (far right) travel from VA to GA for Jessica and
Walker Page's wedding celebration on June 21, 2014. Some of
our FF Group, The Beasleys, Carters, Bowers and Pattersons
are also pictured…friends since Fernbank Elementary!

> Yes, weeping may endure for the night, but JOY does come with the morning."
>
> Psalm 30:5"

Psalm 30:5 came true on the following day as the sun rose on Monday, March 16, 2015, starting with a long phone visit with my grieving friend in Virginia, Kelly, as I walked along the water, stopping in the loveliest places for a moment of quiet reflection and prayer.

One of my many prayer spots in the beautiful
San Diego Embarcadero Bay.

Later, I was thankful to see pictures of my precious Tennessee Tech ADPi sisters loving our friends The Reads, as they represented our group at Taylor's Celebration Service which I was able to watch on livestream.

That afternoon, though his wife, Annie had to work, our nephew, Evan, and their fourteen-month-old son, Noah, were able to drive a short distance to meet us at the beautiful Torrie Pines Reserve. Again, I was struck by irony: grieving with our friends over the loss of their son…while watching this beautiful boy's journey begin.

JOY overflowing as we visited with these two precious ones, my brother John and Jeanie's firstborn and Evan and Annie's firstborn, Noah James Walker, age fourteen months.

As we continue to pray for healing for our Dad, Don, and peace for our friends The Reads, our faith reminds us to be brave.

"For behold, the winter is past; the rain is over and gone. The flowers appear on the earth, the time of singing has come, and the voice of the turtledove is heard in our land."

Song of Solomon 2:11–12

A Related Blog Post

August 20, 2019

5 Reasons We Should Volunteer
Why Should We Do It?

Many may wonder why should we volunteer? When asked about why a group of folks took time out each week to volunteer, the answers were inspiring. To feel needed, to share a skill, to get to know a community different from myself, to demonstrate commitment to a cause or a belief, to gain leadership skills, and to accomplish a civic duty.

(1) Studies have shown that volunteers live longer and healthier lives.

(2) Volunteering can help you establish strong relationships.

(3) Volunteering can complement your career.

(4) Volunteering helps society.

(5) Volunteering gives you a strong sense of purpose.

"Why volunteering makes us healthier is rooted in biology. One of the best ways to get your mind off your aches and pains is to get your mind on someone else," says Stephen Post, coauthor of Why Good Things Happen To Good People: How To Live A Longer, Healthier, Happier Life By The Simple Act Of Giving, and Director of the Center for Medical Humanities, Compassionate Care, and Bioethics at Stony Brook University. This is one of the important lessons my Mama taught me: "When you are down, help someone."

Anyone who has done any amount of volunteering for any measure of time would likely agree that when we give to others with our heart that we can reap benefits which are glorious and unimaginable. Simply being a good listener, expressing joy and humor, or offering a genuine, friendly smile, can contribute to lighting up another person's life. Volunteering can have many surprising benefits!

One cool thing about volunteering is that you can choose an area that you are passionate about. Your love for animals could lead to spending some time helping out at a rescue shelter or a Veterinarian's office. If reading inspires you, spend some time re-shelving books at your local library. Are you an empty nester who misses having little ones in your home, then consider contacting a local indigent hospital, like Grady Memorial Hospital. Here, you may be able to rock babies one afternoon a week. In my recent past, I have chosen The Extension as one of my main volunteer opportunities for Volunteerism since it opened in 2009. The raw courage exhibited by the women who reside there has always challenged me in my personal journey.

Kristen, founder of Kids Boost (www.kidsboost.org) a nonprofit which encourages kids 8-18 to give back to their communities.

In the past, I have met up with the ladies there every other Wednesday and shared an art therapy/collage activity with them. I believe this commitment made a real difference in my life, while encouraging the current Extension residents, as well. My personal desire to give back to the community has been renewed by the fact that I am making a difference, no matter how small.

Oh, and volunteering does not have to be a weekly commitment. It may involve simply providing a meal for a family who is dealing with adversity, join a Mission Team abroad/near home, or simply giving a ride to someone who needs one. Just being on the lookout for who's in your path, you will soon see many ways to lend a hand.

A great example is one my lifelong friend, Jan participates in. Jan told me about it just the other day. The ministry is called Lasagna Love and can be found at www.lasagnalove.org. Their mission is simple.

Feed Families. Spread Kindness. Strengthen Communities.

Studies have shown that volunteering is particularly beneficial to adults age 65 and older, and those who serve more than one hundred hours each year. Volunteers are more likely to report a greater sense of well-being, and of purpose and meaning in their lives, than nonvolunteers. Older adults, who may be prone to social isolation, volunteering can offer strong social networks and a way to stay active in the community. Our parents were a great example of this as volunteers for Meals On Wheels late in their lives.

There has been a debate for some time now regarding whether or not high schoolers should be required to earn a certain number of community service hours. While time management is a real issue, having raised two young adults, we have seen significant benefits of their involvement in their community and beyond. There are many of the positives that can come from your teen being involved in service, whether it is required, or not. I am proud to know eighteen-year-old Aidan, who is on a mission to share the joy and necessity of giving to all. Aidan is a speaker, singer, and songwriter. Aidan's website is www.aidancares.org.

If you haven't gotten involved as a volunteer, why not consider starting today?

YOU CAN MEET THEM
IN SCHOOL,
OR IN LANES,
OR AT SEA,

IN CHURCH,
OR IN TRAINS,
OR IN SHOPS,
OR AT TEA,

FOR THE SAINTS OF GOD
ARE JUST FOLK LIKE ME,
AND I MEAN TO BE ONE, TOO.

Mama encouraged us to help others. However, she knew the most important work she could ever do would happen under her roof, inside the walls of her home.

Mama also knew that staying engaged and involved in the lives of her children and grandchildren was key. This would be the most influential feat she would ever undertake. She noted this in the following journal entry.

From Mama's Journal

April 16, 1981

Here I am on the road again. Last Wednesday, April 14th, Kathy and I left Decatur with the two boys to return to their home in Dandridge, Tennessee. Kathy had to be at work at 10:00 a.m. at Logos Home for Girls. I guess compared to some people, I live an exciting life…it seems it is feast or famine…nothing to do or too much. These past two days have been the golden times.

Time spent with the grandchildren and helping to shape their lives-I always said my favorite time with the children is the first years because all they need is love and care. Now, Luke is ten months old and such a cute age. He is trying to walk. I have enjoyed Shane, too. He is four and a half years old and goes to nursery school where he learns so much.

August 31, 1990
8:28 a.m. Kevin Michael Seder

Kevin is a beautiful baby and Kathy is doing well. Born at Northlake Regional Hospital, Tucker, Georgia. I was in the delivery room. Johnny chose to get the children on the school bus. Joan picked me up at hospital and took me to Kathy's. Jim got Emily and told the children the news of their new brother. Then, we all rested, made calls, made supper for children, then Jim took them to hospital. We all made a tape for John Wade and Jeanie. Good to have the baby here.

From Joan's Journal

November 17, 2011

I am doing both a collage workshop and a Mexican dinner at The Women's Extension tonight! Excited (and honored) to be Jesus' hands and feet to these ladies. Also, my sis, Laura's coming! I have planned an activity with the acronym WATCH.

Watch your Words, Actions, Thoughts, Character, Heart. 'Examine Yourself...'2 Corinthians 13:5a

Before I go, I want to read through a few verses for these five areas:

WORDS: James 3; Eph. 4:29; Note on 3:2-3, 'What you say and what you don't say are both important.'

ACTIONS: 'Let us not love (only) with words or tongue, but with actions and truth.' 1 John 3:18; also 1 Corinthians 10:31

THOUGHTS: Galatians 5:18 'Led by Spirit'; Proverbs 23:12b

CHARACTER: Ephesians 5:15-21; Proverbs 21:21

HEART: All in Proverbs 4:23; 12:25; 17:22; 23:12a; 23:19b

The older I get, the more I realize the preciousness of life. Following my Mama's positive pattern of volunteering has certainly added to the value of my days.

One of Mama's favorite writers and humorists, Erma Bombeck, said it like this:

"When I stand before God at the end of my life, I would hope that I would not have a single bit of talent left, and could say, 'I used everything you gave me.'"

And speaking of the end of life, there are two sure things in life, death and taxes. And believe it or not, sometimes death can be a friend

"No one ever told me that grief felt so much like fear."

C. S. Lewis

"There is a sacredness in tears. They are not the mark of weakness, but of power. They speak more eloquently than ten thousand tongues. They are the messengers of overwhelming grief, of deep contrition, and of unspeakable love."

Washington Irving

Lesson 4

Sometimes, Death Can Be A Friend

My sister just above me in age, Laura Lea recalled this life lesson. Sometimes death can be a friend? What does that even mean? As far as our understanding goes, our Mama's birth mother was killed in a car accident at an early age, and her birth father placed Mama and her two older sisters in an orphanage over concern about his ability to provide for them, especially during The Great Depression.

Mama knew death. She had a keen understanding and acceptance of it, and therefore, believed that "sometimes" it could be a friend.

The C. S. Lewis quote above makes sense. When faced with sudden grief, we may exclaim with fear, "What am I going to do now!?" And then, with the help of friends, family, and God, we begin to put one foot in front of the other. We wade our way in the deep waters before us. One day at a time.

Mom was also known for saying,

"There are many things that are worse than death."

Mama was with several loved ones when they took their last breath. And Laura, along with the rest of us, never would've guessed that Daddy, older than Mama by a few years, would be with his beloved when she took her last breath on October 24, 2006.

Laura Lea, more than her five siblings, has that same keen understanding about death.

Bradford Gordon Lamkie, 1988.

You see, on June 24, 2008, Rhys and Laura's son, Brad was twenty-four when he fell onto the concrete from his six-foot-two height and suffered a TBI. A traumatic brain injury. We knew right away that his injury was acutely serious. Brad went through extensive brain surgery twenty-four hours later. Though Brad did show occasional signs of wakefulness, he never knew us and really showed few significant signs that he would make a recovery. But we, his family, kept hoping and praying. God answered our prayers in a different sort of way… After ten long months, with frequent trips to the emergency room from Signature Healthcare of Buckhead where he was being cared for, Brad passed peacefully in his sleep on Sunday night, April 19, 2009, just after he reached his twenty-fifth birthday. With Rhys and Laura Lea working full-time during this critical and uncertain season, our sister, Mary Ann, and I stepped in visiting with Brad often. Mary Ann and I have reflected on how we both took our Bibles in the hospital for our visits, reading to Brad, making notations in our Bibles, and praying over him. Our family has always believed that comfort, hopefulness, and yes, healing, albeit a heavenly healing at times, is wrought when we align our lives with God and the Scriptures.

Even so, grief is one of the consequences of a life in which one chooses to care, and it reminds us, perhaps more clearly than any other experience, that we are not here alone. Grief is a measure of our humanity. It is the currency of our belonging, the price we pay without reserve. It is our gift to those we have loved that we willingly suffer their loss. Yes, when we love deeply, we grieve much.

Now, you might be saying or at least thinking, how can we "rejoice" over such devastating circumstances? Here are some of the reasons my sister, Laura claims from this heartbreaking experience: God's provision of excellent health care every step of the way; the love, support, and prayers from friends; the realization that when we seek God, we WILL find Him, see James 4:8 and Jeremiah 29:13; the comfort that is provided by food from friends and fellowship with family at a sad time like this. Laura Lea has also expressed to me that one thing we gain from great loss is the astounding ability to observe and notice others in their time of bereavement (see 2 Corinthians 1:3–5).

A clear memory from Brad's childhood also brings tremendous comfort, and likely always will. When Brad and his little sister, Pamela were small, they were allowed to release their seatbelts as they pulled down their short, neighborhood street. Laura has a precious memory of one afternoon when her very small son stood up in the back floorboard of the car, patted her on her shoulders, and said, "Mommy, God talks to me." Even then, God was sowing seeds of faith into this little guy's heart.

I am so very proud of Laura Lea, her husband, Rhys, and Brad's sister, Pamela, as they have traveled through a sudden, unexpected grief journey.

Memories of our gentle-hearted nephew, Brad will live on forever.

As hard as it is to say, our Mama's own death came as a friend. Though it was a brief illness, just one-third of a year, she had suffered greatly with her cancer. In Wellstar Kennestone Hospital for the last ten days on earth, her four daughters, one each night, were able to stay over with her for her final four earthly nights. On Tuesday morning, October 24, 2006, surrounded by her six children, each of their spouses, her Johnny, as well as a sprinkling of grandchildren, Mama took her last breath. Billy recalls one tiny tear dropping from her eye.

When a very sick person passes on, we may see them at their worst. It's an incredibly sacred moment in time. Then friends and family come to share good memories, and it helps ease the pain. It soon became a time of seeing our Mama at her best.

> "When the perishable has been clothed with the imperishable, and the mortal with immortality, then the saying that is written will come true: 'Death has been swallowed up in victory. Where, O death, is your victory? Where, O death, is your sting?"

> 1 Cor. 15:54–55

> "God whispers to us in our pleasures, speaks in our consciences, but shouts in our pains. It is his megaphone to rouse a deaf world."

> C. S. Lewis

The day was February 14, 2010, when Donny, Walker, and I brought Donny's mother, Evelyn Hammett Tunmer to our hometown in Georgia from her home in Fort Pierce, Florida. After the long drive from South Florida to Marietta, Georgia, she was so ill, we had to take her straight to the emergency room, where she was immediately intubated. A nonsmoker her entire life, Evelyn had been diagnosed with metastatic lung cancer. Though we had dreams of her living independently in our community, she was never able to leave Kennestone Hospital. We were with her when she passed on March 6, 2010. When she took her last breath. I held her hand, reading the Twenty-third Psalm aloud. Again, there is something sacred about being with loved ones as they exit this world, entering into eternity. Evelyn was extremely weak and ill.

Death was a friend that day.

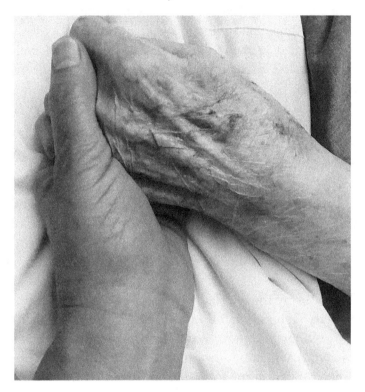

Like my Mama, I have had the honor and privilege to be near the bedsides of many just hours before their final earthly moments. This time of transitioning from life to death is a time one should never have to go at alone.

> "'Tis better to have loved and lost than never to have loved at all."
>
> Alfred Lord Tennyson

As I consider the hallowed passing of those we love so dearly, I have also been thinking of the countless COVID-19 victims who have died without their family. I have nothing but tremendous praise for all of the medical clinicians across this world who have certainly done their best. Still, my heart cries for those who had to hear of a loved one's last breath through FaceTime or a text. When it is our time, it is our time. Still having our people with us is a gift that has not been afforded to many during this worldwide pandemic. For those who have lost loved ones during this pandemic will never know "normal" again.

The day is September 15, 2020. I am alone here in a cottage in the small, quaint town of Port Saint Joe, Florida. The Gulf Coast is in view just outside my front door. The owners, part of our family, have been generous to share this ideal spot with me so that I have an opportunity for writing in solitude. Attempting to keep Hurricane Sally at bay, the winds and rains here are light compared to just west of me in Alabama, Mississippi and Louisiana. Storms are like that, aren't they? We hear about them all the time, but unless we are in the midst of a personal storm, the thought comes and goes as quick as the wind.

That was my thought last night as I watched a newly released documentary about one of my all-time favorite actors, Robin Williams. Oh my gosh, just seeing his name here takes me back to *Mrs. Doubtfire,* Williams fully disguised as a senior woman playing a broom like a guitar in the foyer. I cannot even say how many times I have watched that classic! Appropriately titled "Robin's Wish," Williams' wife, Susan Schneider-Williams did an incredible job explaining the truth of Robin Williams' passing in August 2014.

I remember the year 2014 well. Our two children had just married: Leah and Scott on March 29, 2014; Walker and Jessica on June 21, 2014. In July 2014 we spent a week in Gulf Shores, Alabama, as three married couples. Unforgettable!

Soon after our return, came the story that Williams had passed by suicide due to depression. I know that depression is a clinical condition. Still, I recall thinking…how can someone who makes others' laughter expand to extraordinary extents carry such heavy sorrow in his heart? As I watched this retelling of the circumstances of Robin Williams's life and passing, I became aware of the reality, the truth, the background of his death. You see, from ages sixty-one to sixty-three, Williams was developing the symptoms of Lewy Body Dementia. An incredibly difficult illness to diagnose, over time, this progressive disease can bring on hallucinations, memory issues, movement concerns, and changes in alertness. Heroically and determined, Robin Williams had conquered both addiction and depression earlier in his life journey. Not knowing what this intense third battle was, he strived tirelessly until the end to battle back as he completed recent projects such as a CBS sitcom, *The Crazy Ones*, song with films, *A Merry Friggin' Christmas, The Angriest Man in Brooklyn, and Night at the Museum: Secret of the Tomb* with Ben Stiller and Dick Van Dyke.

His wife, Susan said that his illness was debilitating for Robin and called it "chemical warfare" in his brain. "This disease is like a sea monster with fifty tentacles of symptoms that show when they want," Susan said. "And we can't find it until someone dies definitively. There is no cure."

Please don't misunderstand, I absolutely do not support the work of Dr. Jack Kevorkian, the medical pathologist who is infamously known as "Dr. Death" for his efforts on behalf of assisted suicide. Instead, I carry the belief that a loving, sovereign, caring God determines our steps, as well as our final breath. Still, though no one, but himself assisted Robin Williams in his passing, I can somehow conceive of death being a friend on that day. August 11, 2014, in Paradise, Cay, California when Robin Williams took his leave.

By now, most of us have heard that the Suez Canal was blocked for six days recently between the days of March 23, 2021, until March 29, 2021. It may be surprising how big of an impact this blockage caused. Likewise, circumstances that show up out of the blue can hit us hard and cause life-changing reactions. Since the Suez Canal was completed in 1869, it has been one of the world's most important bodies of water, a portal between East and West that has been controlled by multiple countries. Imagine a mammoth container ship, named *Ever Given*, lodging itself across the waterway. What to do?

About a tenth of global trade passes through here, and the passage could be facing a week-long blockage. What happens when life is interrupted? Some of us can only imagine how grief works when it comes into our life journey without warning. Let's all try our best to exhibit patience toward those who might be suffering through a season of grief. Everyone grieves in their own way and at their own pace. Let's offer grace to ourselves and to others when sorrow shows up at our door. I am learning that I cannot truly know joy unless I have known sorrow.

A Related Blog Post

October 23, 2020

4 Ways To Best Help The Bereaved

As this new month begins, I begin to reflect more than usual on the 14th anniversary of my Mama's passing on October 24, 2006, I want to share here what I have learned are some of the best ways to help those who are grieving. Did you know? The definition of *bereaved* is "to be deprived of a loved one through a profound absence, especially due to the loved one's death.".

"People may excite themselves in a glow of compassion not by toasting their feet at the fire and saying, 'Lord, teach me more compassion,' but by going and seeking a person who needs compassion."

Henry Ward Beecher (1813-1887, an aboli-tionist)

This fall also marks the passing of my Daddy, seven years ago. With both of my parents now gone, I have been encouraged by friends and family, alike.

"We have only this moment, sparkling like a star in our hand…and melting like a snowflake. Let us use it therefore before it is too late."

Marie Edith Beynon

I have grieved with my husband in the passing of his mother in 2010, and then his father just a few years later. We have stood with my sister's family (2009) in the loss of their young adult son, Brad, and more recently we have joined our dear friends in Virginia in the loss of their 23 year old son, Taylor in early 2015. We have stood shoulder-to-shoulder with our dear friends, The Oweida Family with the loss of their young son, our godson Brendan Nizar Oweida. November 4, 2017, pictured here in Elementary School.

In recent years, I have also had the privilege to support others in their grief journeys. A book on grief I have shared with others, that has helped me so much is called A Grace Disguised: How The Soul Grows Through Loss, by Gerald L. Sittser.

4 Ways to Best Help the Bereaved:

(1) Show Up. When you're not sure what to do, simply be there. Those who are grieving want to know you are praying for them and that you care about their loss. This calls for us to reach for courage in order to go to the hard place and love on those in need. Show up with attention and grace.

"The people we love most do become a physical part of us. When we lose them, be it by death or earthly separation, the sense of rupture is real and raw." *Meghan O'Rourke*

(2) Don't worry if you don't have the right words to say. My Mama used to tell me that if I didn't know what to say, it wasn't necessary to say anything, but to be physically present is always important.

(3) Remember them in the weeks and months ahead. Mark your calendar if necessary, to remind yourself to drop them an encouraging note, text, or email. Share your memories of their beloved one. Mail a book, a small gift, or drop some banana bread by their home to let them know their loss has not been forgotten. Many who lose a loved one feel as though everyone else's

life is going on and they are stuck in this place of grief.

Reaching out to them may be just what they need at a particular time.

(4) Speak their name. Never stop saying their loved one's name. Some people may believe that speaking the deceased's name will bring the survivors sadness, but instead there's a good chance it will bring them joy as you remember their loved one by speaking his/her name often.

There are many additional ways to come alongside and encourage those who are grieving.

What are some actions that have helped you during your season of bereavement?

In addition to writing her thoughts, Mama also copied poems, quotes, and excerpts from books into her journals. Like the entry below about Love.

From Mama's Journal

September 24, 1985

"Never doubt love, never question it when it comes on stage. Instead, be happy for its entrance. And do not weep when it makes its exit, for it leaves behind the sweet aroma of caring. A fragrance to linger the rest of your life."

From A Necessary Woman by, Helen Van Slyke

From Joan's Journal

Wednesday, March 17, 2021

The day is March 17, 2021. I am home in Marietta on this rainy, cool Wednesday. My heart has been heavy with the June 2020, lung cancer diagnosis of my neighbor and friend, Sherri, two doors down. Never a smoker, grandmother to three precious boys, and my same age. Under the care of Hospice, this friend is drawing to the end of her earthly life. Even though we have lived here a much shorter time than these neighbors, she and I connected immediately, becoming fast friends. Kindred spirits.

I just walked down to take some cookies for her grandsons and had a chance to visit with her husband, Tim, on the porch for a few minutes. As he held and snuggled with our new pup, Cami, we talked about how sad this season is. How sacred this season is. With tears in his eyes, he shared how thankful he was that his wife was not fearful, and had instead, expressed "readiness" to him. He bravely added,

"She'll just get there before we do."

Her husband, her son, her daughter, their 3 small grandsons and families all have to courageously say, "See you later." They will have an angel watching over them until they meet again.

Friday, March 26, 2021

The Celebration of Life for Sherri McClendon O'Kelley service was held at 4:00 p.m. today, at a church on the Historical Marietta Square. Donny and I walked from our home to attend. What a beautiful service, it was. The music, the friends sharing and most of all the bravery shown by Sherri's married children, Sean and Shannon, when they spoke. They told the congregation all they had learned from their Mom through the years. Especially in the past ten months while she fought cancer.

Sherri and her fun-loving family. December 2020.

A heavenly healing is sometimes what comes. We don't always understand. Still, we walk by faith, not by sight. We trust that there is truth in the verse, 'absent from the body is present with the Lord'. His peace will guard this family's life until they meet again.

My friend's godly confidence reminds me of a conversation between Mama and Mary Ann back in 2006. They were on the way to the hospital, unknowingly for the last ten days of Mama's earthly life. On the way, she said, "I have my bags packed." Mama was expressing the same eagerness as my friend. An acceptance, a trust of the promise in 2 Corinthians 5:8, "Yes, we are fully confident, and we would rather be away from

these earthly bodies, for then we will be at home
with the Lord."

The morning following our porch visit,
I received this text from my new friend's husband: "Joan, Sherri entered Glory last night. Our
daughter had made it home and was able to see
her, thank goodness. Now Sherri is healed, no
more pain."

Another Related Blog Post

November 14, 2013

A Loving Eulogy for My Father
November 11th Veteran's Day 2013

'Tis better to have loved and lost than never
to have loved at all." Alfred Lord Tennyson,
British Poet (1809-1892) from his poem "In
Memoriam A.H.H."

Five years ago on November 11, 2013, my
Daddy passed away and went to join my Mama.
It was Veteran's Day, which was appropriate since
Daddy had served in the U.S. Army Medical
Corps in the late 1940s. My five siblings and I
came up with the following attributes in refer-
ence to our father:

God-inspired, man of character, compassionate, humble, man of stability, respectable,
charming, hard worker, steadfast family man,
musician, avid fisherman, and beloved physician.

Daddy as a young doctor serving in the bush of Africa, 1951

At the age of 93, it was certainly evident to each one of us that he had lived a long and beautiful life. Even so, this has not changed the truth of how much we miss him and our Mama, too. When one loves completely, the "missing" may lessen, but it never goes away. Following are the words I spoke at Daddy's funeral, with my brother, Billy standing beside me. This was my message to honor the memory of my beloved father:

JOAN'S EULOGY FOR HER DADDY
NOVEMBER 14, 2013

Our father slipped away quietly on Monday, a gorgeous, autumn afternoon. The kind of day that our mom would've loved. When author C.S. Lewis' wife passed away, he was quoted as saying:

"Her absence is like the sky, spread over everything."

C.S. Lewis (1898-1963) quote from his book, A Grief Observed, written in 1960

I believe that is exactly how our Dad felt after our Mama's brief illness and death in October 2006. In fact, some of us thought Dad may join her in that first year of his bereavement. Perhaps dying of a broken heart. But instead, our strong and courageous father rallied. Daddy continued to play his clarinet for his grandchildren. He took take daily walks for fitness at nearby Dellinger Park. Dad also resumed his volunteer position of delivering Meals on Wheels to the homebound.

From the time I was a little girl, our big family drove to Savannah Beach every August for our annual family vacation. Often this trip landed on my birthday and I thought that was just part of the plan. A beach birthday trip for Joan and family!

These were always great times! It was wonderful to see Daddy relax and take a break from his busy OB-Gyn solo practice.

When I think about who I am today, and who I am becoming, I think of both my mother and my father. Some of the most important character traits instilled in myself, my brothers, and my sisters are compassion and a strong work ethic. We now observe these same traits and many more in their grandchildren. WE are all thankful for the role model given to us by our parents, and I hope all of us for generations to come will honor their memory with our own lives.

Another life lesson that my father taught me is to have equanimity. A mental or emotional stability or composure, especially under tension or strain; calmness. While I am definitely still learning to practice equanimity, I believe another way to think of this is in Psalm 46:10:

"Be still and know that I am God."

In closing, I remember how special the fall season has been to our parents. Their wedding was on October 21, 1948. Both Mom and Dad have now had their Homegoing in the fall.

I am reminded of one of Dad's favorite musicians, Frank Sinatra, singing:

Autumn Leaves

"Since you went away the days grow long,
And soon I'll hear old winter's song.
But I miss you, most of all my darling,
When autumn leaves start to fall."

I love you Mama and Daddy, so glad you're finally back together!

These thoughts on death cause us to pause and to think about our last day, don't they?

It is both ultimately and intimately between each created human and God. Where are you and I in our journey today? How is there inward, outward and upward evidence of faith in our lives today?

"Despite the fact that I had been a Christian for many years before the accident, since then, God has become a living reality to me as never before. My confidence in God is somehow quieter but stronger. I feel little pressure to impress God or prove myself to him; yet I want to serve him with all my heart and strength. My life is full of bounty, even as I continue to feel the pain of loss. Grace is transforming me, and it is wonderful. I have slowly learned

where God belongs and have allowed him to assume that place—at the center of life rather than at the periphery."

Gerald L. Sittser, author of A Grace Disguised

What Cancer Cannot Do

Cancer is so limited…it cannot cripple love.
It cannot shatter hope.
It cannot corrode faith.
It cannot eat away peace.
It cannot destroy confidence.
It cannot kill friendship.
It cannot shut out memories.
It cannot silence courage.
It cannot reduce eternal life.
It cannot quench the Spirit.

Dr. Robert L. Lyon

As we journey on through Mama's Life Lessons, it is easy to recognize that life is truly a series of variabilities, uncertainties paired with constant change. When times get tough, we might just fall down.

Mama always said, if you find yourself down, you may as well pray.

"In faith there is enough light for those who want to believe and enough shadows to blind those who don't."

Blaise Pascal (1623-1662) a French mathematician, physicist, inventor, writer, and Christian philosopher, Pascal had poor health especially after his 18th year and his death came just two months after his 39th birthday.

Lesson 5

When You Fall Down, You May as Well Pray

Have you ever fallen down? Most of us can give a resounding "yes!" to that question. Life throws us curve balls sometimes, and whether you have fallen down physically or figuratively, it is definitely not fun. One of the few guarantees in life is that it will not turn out the way we expect. Our lives are complex and demanding enough. When we fall, times grow even more challenging. Mama taught us to fall to our knees when unexpected circumstances came around, and to seek God, claiming his over seven thousand promises in the Word.

Mama fell now and then, and one of her favorite sayings was, "If you're already on the ground, you may as well pray." There is no question that parenting keeps you on your knees and I am quite sure the six of us kept Mama praying much of the time, whether she was on the ground or not.

Adopted by Pastor Evan Bishop Shivers and his wife, Maxine, little Polly was immediately a younger sister to three handsome big brothers, Bud, Tom, and Bob, all birth children of The Shivers. The story I heard growing up is that Rev. Shivers, along with a deacon of the church was visiting the orphanage where Mama lived. When Pastor Shivers saw, her, he scooped up that three-year-old little girl and took her home. On the way, they stopped for chocolate ice cream, which of course, dribbled all down her little white toddler dress. Maxine Shivers apparently had no idea that she was about to be a mother to not three, but four, starting that Sunday afternoon. Mama's birth name was "Jo Nelle," but that day her new daddy named her Polly, and she went by Polly from then on.

Mama with her parents: Maxine Dickerson Shivers and Pastor
E. B. Shivers, Maxie and Pappy to all of us, 1948.

Now, a "PK," a preacher's kid, Mama would grow up going to church every time the doors were open. Her brothers, Maxie and Rev. Shivers, known as Pappy to all of us, loved our Mama so much and showed her the way to God's love too. Mama considered her landing into this family as one of her greatest blessings. Mom recognized the gift she had received to be the baby of four in this love-filled household, and she lived the rest of her days with gratefulness in her heart.

The Shivers Family has been an incredibly special part of our lives! Uncle Bud, Mama's brother even officiated at all four of our weddings: Mary Ann and Jim's, Kathy and Jim's, Laura Lea and Rhys's and ours.

Firstborn daughter, Mary Ann lovingly recalls Mama as having an authentic faith and practicing it by serving and loving those around her. Whether she was serving home-baked cakes, provided by the ladies in our church, to the injured veterans at our local VA Hospital or ladling out soup for one of our long-haired hippy-ish boyfriends, she loved unconditionally and without judgment.

And even though Daddy couldn't attend regularly because of his rigorous work schedule, Mama made sure we were in church. Located at the intersection of Scott Boulevard and North Decatur Road, our Scott Boulevard Church Family was a vital and impressionable part of our growing up years. Vacation Bible School where we lined up by age next to the busy highway, Wednesday night suppers, Training Union, and GA's were integral ways the truth was implanted into our beings. On Sunday mornings, we would sleepily file into the building filling up the last pew in the sanctuary, our "assigned" seat.

The oldest of what became known as The Walker Clan, John Wade, observed that our Mama had very little fear because she prayed daily, read her Bible, and was comfortable speaking her mind when others asked her opinion, and sometimes when they didn't. Did you know? The Bible commands us to "fear not" 365 times, one for each day of the year. Her prayers led Daddy and Mama to support Medical Organizations which believed in the sanctity of birth conception.

> If you don't believe in miracles, perhaps you've forgotten you are one.
>
> Anonymous

For you formed my inward parts; you knit me together in my mother's womb. I praise you, for I am fearfully and wonderfully made. Wonderful are your works; my soul knows it very well.

Psalm 139:13–14

And we know that in all things God works
for the good of those who love him, who have
been called according to his purpose."

Romans 8:28

Mama is now in the glory of Heaven with our father who joined
her on November 11, 2013. Likely regularly rocking babies.

Mama's daily regimen of prayer impacted all who crossed paths
with her, most especially her husband and six children. Just as we
read in Proverbs 31:10–31, Mama was far more valuable than rubies,
our Daddy had full trust in her, she was good to him rather than evil,
she worked hard with her hands, she rose early to meet the needs
of her big family, she served those less fortunate, she did not fear
the future, she was strong, honorable, kind, wise, forever watching
over our household, her children call her blessed, her husband always
praised her, she feared only our God, and in complete humility,
Mama allowed her works to speak for themselves.

Falling down can often mean traveling through a life storm,
some sort of adversity. We can all relate to that! While a student at
Fernbank Elementary, I was placed in the lowest learning group. As
a teacher, I understand the importance of dividing students according to their learning pace. These four groups, however, were north
(highest), south (lowest), with east and west in between. A little too
obvious. I can easily recall the way I felt, especially since my friends
were placed higher. This experience definitely affected how I felt
about myself, in a negative way. Children are like sponges, so impressionable. While we cannot and should not rescue our young from the
difficult times they might face, it is critical to teach them which way
to turn when faced with hardship. Prayer in a loving, caring Father is
a place to turn. Modeling this, like my Mama did, will work wonders
for the littles in our lives. At some point, I recall seeing an old-fash-
ioned cross-stitch sampler in someone's kitchen, that said this so well:
"When your day is hemmed with prayer, it's less likely to unravel."

One of my greatest blessings in this life is my small group Bible
Study that has been meeting in Sara Rives Spickler's home for twenty

years, since 2001. Many of us had been studying The Word together for years in BSF, Bible Study Fellowship (www.bsfinternational.org) where for more than sixty years, men, women, students, and children have studied chapter by chapter under trained group leaders, at no costs to the student. Most of our children, as preschoolers attended BSF. This four-fold approach emphasizes the study of Holy Scripture to know God, and to then, apply His Truth.

A few years following the passing of Sara's first husband, Dr. Douglas A. Rives on November 30, 1996, Sara decided to start a small study within her home. Now a single Mom with three young children, Sara knew the added support and accountability would be beneficial. And it has been, so very much! And not just for Sara.

The ten of us support one another through prayer, weekly study, meals when we need them, and life support for the journey. Our group, over time, has become a solid group of prayer warriors. I am grateful for the friendship I share with each one: Sara, Donna, Ansley, Debbie, Marian, Trish, Donalee, Susanna, and Cathy.

Sara and Joan, 2001.

From Mama's Journal

August 29, 1982

Jeanie is in labor! 3:00 p.m. Mary Ann just came out and Jeanie is 3-4 cm and doing really well.

Savannah Lea Walker Born! She is beautiful!

October 3, 1983

I cannot believe I did not finish the above entry. Life got really busy after Savannah's birth and I simply did not write!

This is a day for my soul to catch up with my body. We are at Joel's Lake. I am relaxing while Johnny fishes. So much has happened since I last wrote! I don't know where to begin, so I will start with this A.M. Johnny and I slept well, got up had Bfk and got him off to work. Called Mary Alice first. They returned home about 11:00 p.m. last night. She sounded good, and I know she will be fine. Time always helps to heal. Talked to Bob, too, and he is okay. Losing a brother is a big loss for our family. Talked with Kathy and she is busy as usual. Called Tom and Ann, they returned home O.K. Mary Ann called, too. When Amy got up, she put on THREE pairs of pants! Jim caught a 3-foot King and lots of other fish. Johnny came home for lunch and then we left to fish. This is a beautiful October day. Blue sky, no clouds. Green, yellow, red leaves, cool breeze, the sounds in the distance are airplanes, saws, cows, crows, along with other birds. This is a very restful place, however, the fish are not biting today. I feel so lazy. I just had to write a few things down. My mind is so full. I cannot concentrate on the novel I am reading.

My brother Bud died on September 1st in his sleep and it was a shock to us because he regained his health after being so sick last January. We went to Ackerman for funeral. It was a sad occasion, but a celebration of Eternal Life!

We are so thankful Bud was able to officiate all four of our girls' weddings. What a gift!

From Joan's Journal

July 25, 2014

Both of our children are now married! The six of us just spent the week at Beach Club, Bristol Tower, Unit 910. This is the Gulf Shores, AL unit we owned for seven years when Leah and Walker were younger, between 2000-2007. Time goes by! Walker and Jessica will move to St. Louis, MO in just one week! We will miss them so much, however, we are happy they are going after their dreams together. Walker will be in PhD school at SLU and Jess will be a practicing nurse at Barnes Jewish Hospital. Leah and Scott are also settling into their life, together, now married for four months. We're glad they live near us! Leah works in the Marketing Department for Wellstar Hospital System, and Scott is employed by Zimmer, a medical device company. It feels fantastic to have two happily married children. We have been praying for their partners since they were infants. God has answered our prayers in a wonderful way!

Laura Lea remembers fondly, as she talked with Mom through the years, she would tell her, "Mom, you are so wise, and you know more than I will ever know."

Our quarterly Sister Session! Love this special time with my three sisters. Always feel like Mama is sitting there with us.

Mom's response was always the same, "You will someday." Now someday is here, and we still have a way to go, but my sisters and I are evolving and slowly becoming wise women, like our mother.

Thankfully, discernment truly does come with age, so I bet you are growing in wisdom as well.

My sisters are some of my greatest prayer partners. We try to meet for "A Sister Session" every two to three months. These visits add such richness to our lives. When we are together, we see Mama in our gestures, our smiles, our words, our laughter.

When we fall down. When unexpected and challenging circumstances arise, will we attempt to solve our problems on our own, or will we simply look up and seek God?

A Related Blog Post

October 8, 2019

Fertile Prayers

As we celebrate our first-born's 31st birthday today, I am sharing this unforgettable story of how Leah came to be. Since this story played out in 1987-1988, my God has given me many reasons to be a person of hope and gratitude.

Many may wonder how it feels to be a mother of a 31-year-old daughter, a 27-year-old son, as well as a new grandmother to two two-year-olds.

My main thought is one of pure joy and gratefulness that we are all still here to celebrate this day! We've all heard it said that "gratitude is a game changer in one's attitude and approach to everyday living", and I believe this with all of my heart!

Cheers to Leah Page Andrews today, October 8th!

Wishing you many, many more birthdays in the years ahead!

As a teacher at Avondale Elementary and a few years of suffering with unexplained infertility, I was near my wit's end. We had planned it all out perfectly, hadn't we? With my husband still in the midst of his many years of medical training, we were hoping for a Spring baby. This way I could connect my maternity leave with a nice long summer before returning to the classroom.

With May 1987, came another season of sadness and despair as we had one after another negative pregnancy test. It seemed that everyone we knew was having their first or second child. Married for five years, this was a season of adversity in our marriage. We both wondered aloud and privately if we would ever have the privilege of being parents. During my 1987-1988 Christmas Break, I found myself pleading with my God more than ever before.

I cross-stitched Romans 8:28 and placed it in a frame.

"And we know that in all things God works for the good of those who love him, who have been called according to his purpose."

Soon after this, a snow-filled, early January Monday kept my husband and me home from work. We built a roaring fire and played Canasta, taking in the delight of an unexpected break from work.

Overjoyed to have this serendipitous holiday together, we would later discover that this day was likely the day that our first-born child was at long last conceived.

(sorry for the TMI: *too much information*<smile>)

Some of the lessons we learned from this experience are:

Joan with firstborn, Leah. 1989.

- God's timing is perfect.
- God knows even better than we know what is best for us.
- Adversity makes us stronger. We must stick together even when things get tough.
- When we seek God, we will find Him. In adversity, He draws us into a deeper walk with Him.

Leah and Michael Scott Andrews' wedding day! March 29, 2014.

Brother Billy and Joan, October 2, 1982.

- God hears our pleas.

Leah with firstborn, Tripp, 2020.

Another Related Blog Post

March 13, 2017

Authentic Prayer
A Continual Conversation
Does it make any difference to pray?

Maya Angelou has a quote about prayer that I find myself reflecting on often:

"I know that when I pray, something wonderful happens. Not just to the person or persons for whom I'm praying, but also something wonderful happens to me. I'm grateful that I'm heard."

You know, the older I get, the more I realize the massive need I have for prayer in my life journey. It's been said that getting old isn't for sissies and it's not for the faint of heart either!

Did you know? Praying is easier than you might imagine. God is faithful and gracious.

His mercies towards us as His children are brand new with each new day.

I want to follow that age-old verse found in First Thessalonians Chapter Five:

"Rejoice always, pray without ceasing, in everything give thanks; for this is the will of God in Christ Jesus for you."

1 Thessalonians 5:16-18

For me that means to maintain a grateful heart regardless of my circumstances. To carry on a continual conversation with my Creator. It also means I yearn to keep a short list of my wrongdoings as He lovingly convicts me and brings them to my mind and heart. I truly believe that prayer makes a big difference in my personal life journey.

And we are in the middle of the Lent Season where believers choose to say "no" as a gift to God…a way to purify themselves during this penitential season. So, it's a perfect season to ponder the purpose and place of prayer in your life and in mine.

One of the most helpful books I have ever read about this is Help, Thanks, Wow: The Three Essential Prayers by, Anne Lamott.

I recently ran across an anonymous prayer from the 17th Century, "A Nun's Prayer." Transparent and honest prayers such as this are received and valued by God. He is listening. Are we talking to Him? Are we listening out for His still small voice? He wants to hear from us, and He covets a personal relationship with you and with me.

"Lord, Thou knowest better than I know myself that I am growing older and will be someday old. Keep me from the fatal habit of thinking I must say something on every subject and on every occasion. Release me from craving to straighten out everybody's affairs. Make me thoughtful but not moody. Helpful, but not bossy with my vast store of wisdom; it seems a pity not to use it all, but Thou knowest, Lord, that I want a few friends at the end. Keep my mind free from the recital of endless details; give me wings to get to the point swiftly. Seal my lips on my aches and pains. They are increasing, and love of rehearsing them is becoming sweeter as the years go by. I dare not ask for grace enough to enjoy the tails of others' pains but help me to endure them with patience. I dare not ask for improved memory, but for a growing humility and a lessening cocksureness when my memory seems to clash with the memories of others. Teach me the glorious lesson that I occasionally may be mistaken. Keep me reasonably sweet; I do not want to be a sour old person. Some of them are so hard to live with and each one a crowning work of the devil. Give me the ability to see good things in unexpected places, and talents in unexpected people. And give me, O Lord, the grace to tell them so. Amen."

"It is God who arms me with strength and makes my way perfect. He makes my feet like the feet of a deer; He enables me to stand on the heights."

2 Samuel 22:33-34

"She who kneels before God can stand before anyone." Romans 8:31

What part does prayer have in your life journey? Did you know? There are many verses that tell us that when we choose to see God, we will find Him every time. I have definitely found this to be true for me...every time.

If you and I find we do not feel close to God, Creator, guess who moved?

Let's get the conversation going!

More favorite books about prayer:

Prayer: Does It Make Any Difference? by Philip Yancey

Prayer: The Ultimate Conversation by, Charles F. Stanley

Prayer: Experiencing Awe and Intimacy with God by, Tim Keller

Fervent: A Woman's Battle Plan for Serious, Specific, and Strategic Prayer by, Priscilla Shirer

before AMEN: The Power of a Simple Prayer by, Max Lucado

As I shared earlier, I have always loved writing things down. Over time, I have journaled, recorded prayers from my heart, made notations in cookbooks, and penned loads of letters to my friends and family. Yes, I learned this from Mama, as well. Next, we will see how she loved communicating through the lost art of letter writing. Mama additionally accentuated reading books as we were coming up. Billy recalled Mama planting herself in a comfortable chair, as we circled around her for story time. We had so many books in our Webster Drive basement that

Daddy made us organize them according to the Dewey Decimal System, 000 all the way to 900! An entire wall of bookshelves.

Reading and Writing. I cannot imagine my life without these two positive pursuits.

"To send a letter is a good way to go somewhere
without moving anything but your heart."

Phyllis Theroux, author of The Journal Keeper

"Take some books and read; that's an immense help; and
books are always good company if you have the right sort."

Louisa May Alcott, Little Women

"A person recently bereaved of an only sister, wrote to a friend:
'Isn't it wonderful that the really fine things in life are not things
at all. And so it is. Love, friendship, appreciation, kindness,
honesty, thrift, and a multitude of life's finest qualities, are
intangible and spiritual. But nevertheless, very real.'" Anonymous

Lesson 6

Read Books. Write Letters.

Mama loved to read books and she instilled into all six of her children that same love. Her passion for reading was real and contagious. She loved the newspaper, too, because as a busy mom, she felt like this was a way to stay connected to current events. Visiting the public library in downtown Decatur was a common occurrence for our family. My siblings have shared that they did the same thing when their children were coming up…story times at the library give tired moms a few minutes to catch their breath.

Mama read anything she could get her hands on. She often shared that she felt like reading was a way to "travel" to places she may never have the chance to visit. I agree.

What kind of books do you like to read? I enjoy memoirs and historical fiction. I will be forever inspired by true-life stories where adversity has been conquered by the human spirit. Overcomers provide a great catalyst for self-improvement.

Who writes personal letters anymore? What with emails, Instagram, Twitter, and Facebook all as options to stay connected.

The thing is a letter or card which someone took the time to write, stamp, and mail to you can be held in your hands and reread again and again, unlike any of these other means of communication. When you check your mailbox, does your heart skip a beat when you see an item of personal mail? Mine does, and I believe most would agree that it feels good to be remembered by another person.

> "One of my favorite times to write letters is when I am on a long trip. Whether I am traveling by car, plane, ship, or train, I pull together everything I need and place my materials in a zippered pouch."
>
> Joan W Page

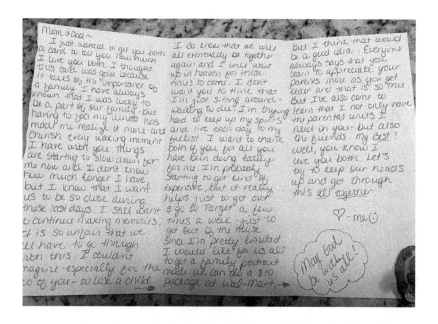

Christy Buice (as mentioned in lesson 2) wrote this letter to her parents, Dixie and Benny just months before she passed away at age twenty-one from Ewing Sarcoma, 1999. Christy was strong and courageous. She shared her bravery with her parents and close friends by writing letters they could keep forever.

A handwritten note is still one of the simplest, most wonderful gifts I can receive. No text or email can replace the personal touch that comes from the hand, the paper, the pen, the heart.

At Mama's Celebration Service on October 26, 2006, the pastor asked the congregation of two hundred–plus how many folks had received a card or a letter from Miss Polly. Nearly every person raised their hand.

Mama had a ministry, and she knew it was impacting others.

From Mama's Journal

Monday, September 29, 1986

We arrived at the Kinshasa Airport at 8:30-9:30. We were tired from our travels, but oh so excited. After three decades since my last trip to Africa, it felt like coming home again. We soon fell into bed at the guest house until the rooster crowed at 5:30 a.m. He thinks he owns the yard! After getting settled, we had the chance to reconnect with many of our friends from the fifties when we served here. I have been washing our clothes and hanging them in the sun to dry. We visited the beautiful School Complex. This was started twenty-five years ago for the missionary children. Now, they have 536 students. We are enjoying the delicious foods here, mango, avocado paste, potato soup, papaya, and pomegranate. We are careful to boil our water before drinking.

We visited Sona Bata, where Mary Ann was born, and saw the many changes.

I have just mailed letters to all the children, to Tom and Ann, and also to Bob. I have the mail pouch ready to go back to church.

January 2, 1987

Quote for the New Year: "Time to reflect on the year that's just past. Time to make plans for new joys that will last."

Johnny is having a lot of trouble with his eye, a possible detached retina. We will go to town to have it checked. We got letters from Joe and Ben D. & Ina F. and Frank.

January 4, 1987

This is the day we will try to make our reservations. "Human action can be modified to some extent, but human nature cannot be changed."
A. Lincoln
'We need your help, Lord, as we make our travel plans. You know we will follow your leading for our lives, and place our lives in your hands, as always.'
This has been a wonderful "Mountain Top Experience."
I have no regrets except for a selfish disappointment.

Note: After Mama and Daddy became empty nesters, they sold their home in Decatur, Georgia and headed back to serve in The Democratic Republic of the Congo. Plans were to serve for a full year or more, returning to the bush in the heart of Africa. Because of unforeseen health issues with Daddy's eye, their trip only lasted around four months.

From Joan's Journal

Tuesday, November 8, 2011

When I wrote to Walker this morning, I told him I was praying Psalm 1 for he and Jess this week. It's hard to believe they are both now Sophomores in college! I know it must be hard to keep up their long-distance relationship. Donny and I dated from afar for about a year. I was just reading an exposition on Psalm 1 by Charles Spurgeon. 'It is a rich sign of inward grace when the outward walk is changed, and when ungodliness is put far from our actions.' As I read and study this, I am so very thankful that I know the Shepherd, and He knows, loves me, too. (despite my daily shortcomings) Of that, I am sure! While I am very far from being faultless, (actually, there is no such thing as perfection) I clearly understand the significant LIFE message in the words I copied above from Spurgeon's book. Thank You, Jesus.

My friend, Sherri O'Kelley's four-bedroom walls were layered with encouraging, life-giving messages during her illness.

Mom even had a pen pal relationship with a young man named Mark who was in the Georgia State Prison. We have several letters that Mark sent to her after she had written to him. A foster child since he was young, his letters are filled with thankfulness that she cared. From one of Mark's letters dated April 14, 2004: "Dear Mrs.

Polly, I just wanted to say thank you for the birthday card and all of the cards that you take the time to send to me. I am doing okay."

Mama's letters, no doubt brightened his days in prison. To express his gratitude, Mark created little white angels with the art of crochet, a skill he learned during his incarceration. After Mark mailed these to Mama, she shared them with all of us. With her gift came a reminder to pray for Mark's future ahead.

I don't know about you, but I recall being very homesick when I went away to college, especially at first. Mama wrote to me consistently during my four years away in school, first at Tennessee Tech University where I spent my initial two undergraduate years, and then at the University of Georgia. She wrote to all six married couples during the ten years they spent in retirement in Mississippi. In May 1988, when I was a few months pregnant with our firstborn, the following came to our mailbox:

> Take care of yourselves, and don't work too hard.
> Let us know as soon as soon as you know your plans.
> You know we love you very much.
>
> Mom and Dad

One might think that with me being #5 that she would be a bit weary of writing, but she enjoyed it immensely. The recipient of her kindness always felt loved and appreciated. Again, her six children have followed her example as we all enjoy communicating through the written word.

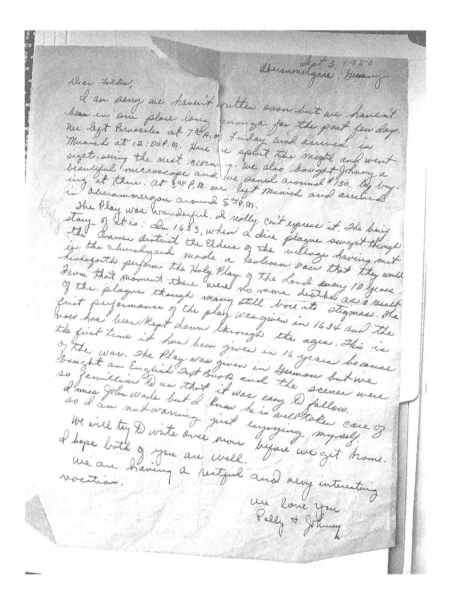

In lesson 2, I shared with you about how delighted she was to have been able to be present for not just one, but three international renditions of *The Passion Play*.

Here is a letter Mama penned to Daddy's parents on September 3, 1950, written from Oberammergau.

When my big brother, John Wade was serving as a Marine Corps in Operation Desert Shield, he wrote the following in a December 25, 1990 letter to home:

> Mail is truly the lifeblood of our morale here,
> and I am certainly very appreciative of
> all the letters, packages, etc.
> Christmas is what you carry in your heart,
> and now I am happy and content because
> I realize how much my family and friends
> love and have personal concern about my
> present welfare. Positive memories of Jeanie,
> our children, our parents, family members and
> life-long friendships remain strong in my mind
> and continue to provide a
> resilience of strength and perseverance.

This shows the importance of letters and care packages going out regularly to our military men and women. Thanks to my high school friend, Nancy, I have been fortunate to be a part of a group that sends Christmas packages to our military. As a military mom, Nancy has been good about using social media to keep the word out about servicemen and women who need our love and prayers. Google "300 Boogle Brigade" to learn more. Mama always reminded us that they were the very ones who serve to protect our freedom. Supporting them brings joy and encouragement to these soldiers, as well as to their family back home.

Even though my sis, Laura Lea only lives an hour or so from me, we still write letters to each other. We sometimes carry an incomplete letter around in our purse or journal, knowing we will add a new date soon and offer another entry. We have named this "a pocket letter." One we carry around, adding our thoughts as they come, until there is no more space on the page. At that time, we know that it is time to put a stamp on it and send it off.

One of my favorite times to write letters is when I am on a long trip. Whether I am traveling by car, plane, ship, or train, I pull together everything I need and place my materials into a zippered pouch. Included are stamps, envelopes addressed to my recipients, return labels, greeting cards or notecards that I like, and a few favorite black ink pens. Once settled in my seat, I can write letter after letter. It is such pleasure to deposit the collection into a big blue mailbox once I reach my destination.

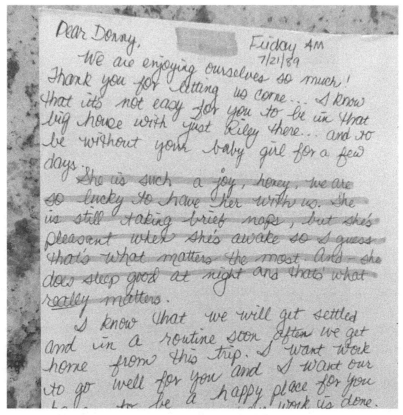

A letter written to Donny in 1989 from my parent's home in Mississippi, his first time away from our firstborn, Leah Suzanne.

I truly hope that reading books and writing letters never go out of style.

What choices can you and I make to be sure that they don't!?!

A Related Blog Post

May 11, 2020

Letter Challenge
Send One Today

I have a letter writing challenge for you today. This past March 4, 2021 would have been my Daddy's 101st birthday!

Among many other things, Johnny Walker was known for gentleness, kindness, wisdom, and love letters.

Mama's engagement picture, 1948.

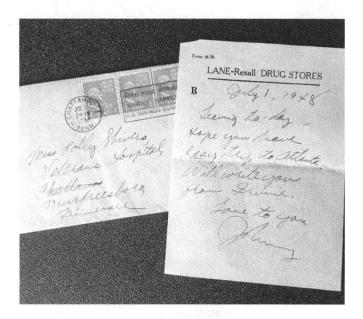

Here is a short love letter he mailed to my Mama just a few months before they wed in October 1948, with a promise to write again when he reached his hometown of Irvine, Kentucky.

I cannot help but believe that small acts like sending this note to his fiancé added up to great love among themselves, their children, grandchildren, great-grands, and the multitudes they crossed paths with during their 58-year marriage. Now they are together forever!

The challenge is simple. Instead of the usual texts and emails, let's challenge each other to surprise the special people in our lives with handwritten love notes. These can be sent or mailed to grandchildren, best girlfriends, collegiates, young marrieds, parents, and more.

For those you share a home with, a short note can be left for them to find in a lunchbox, under their pillow, on a bathroom mirror, on a car seat, slipped in a suitcase for the traveler, or by the coffee maker.

Like my Daddy's example, it doesn't have to be long. The message will provide affirmation, a reminder of your love, and emotional support for the recipient.

I am quite sure you are aware of the passing of Mrs. Nancy Reagan, wife of our 40th U.S. President, Ronald Reagan in March 2016. President Reagan was also known for sending love letters to his sweetheart.

I am currently reading a historical fiction book The Postmistress by, Sarah Blake set in both London and coastal Franklin, Massachusetts. This intriguing novel based on details of the early 1940's really got me thinking about the importance of personal letters.

And it does not have to be a full letter! How about leaving behind post-it notes for the ones you love the most.

The Way of Love 1 Corinthians 13 The Message

1 If I speak with human eloquence and angelic ecstasy but don't love, I'm nothing but the creaking of a rusty gate.

2 If I speak God's Word with power, revealing all his mysteries and making everything plain as day, and if I have faith that says to a mountain, "Jump," and it jumps, but I don't love, I'm nothing.

3-7 If I give everything I own to the poor and even go to the stake to be burned as a martyr, but I don't love, I've gotten nowhere. So, no matter what I say, what I believe, and what I do, I'm bankrupt without love.
Love never gives up.

Love cares more for others than for self.
Love doesn't want what it doesn't have.
Love doesn't strut,
Doesn't have a swelled head,
Doesn't force itself on others,
Isn't always "me first,"
Doesn't fly off the handle,
Doesn't keep score of the sins of others,
Doesn't revel when others grovel,
Takes pleasure in the flowering of truth,
Puts up with anything,
Trusts God always,
Always looks for the best,
Never looks back,
But keeps going to the end.

8-10 Love never dies. Inspired speech will be over some day; praying in tongues will end; understanding will reach its limit. We know only a portion of the truth, and what we say about God is always incomplete. But when the Complete arrives, our incompletes will be canceled.

11 When I was an infant at my mother's breast, I gurgled and cooed like any infant. When I grew up, I left those infant ways for good.

12 We don't yet see things clearly. We're squinting in a fog, peering through a mist. But it won't be long before the weather clears and the sun shines bright! We'll see it all then, see it all as clearly as God sees us, knowing him directly just as he knows us!

13 But for right now, until that completeness, we have three things to do to lead us toward that consummation: Trust steadily in God, hope unswervingly, love extravagantly. And the best of the three is love.

Who will you send a note or letter to today? Make a list of your five favorite books. Share these titles with friends and family.

Pop reads a story to Elizabeth and Tripp (2020) at Lakehaven two.

LESSON 6

Another Related Blog Post

May 24, 2016

Read It Loud
How To Make A Connection

Earlier today, on Tuesday, I was reading aloud to my father-in-law, Don. His across the hall neighbor, Bob at Daybreak Village in Kennesaw, Georgia joined us for the reading time. Having always loved reading to Leah and Walker, I discovered, once again, that reading aloud is a great way to make a connection with another beating heart. I hope by the time you finish this short post, that you, too, will be inspired to share reading with someone in your world.

Back in the mid-1970s, I was a highschooler when I would drive myself to Wesley Woods Retirement Community to visit my paternal grandmother, Anna Mae Walker, known as Mamaw to all of us.

> "Dying is only one thing to be sad over. Living unhappily is something else."
>
> *Morrie Schwartz to Mitch in*
> *Tuesdays With Morrie*

Mamaw had been widowed for well over a decade and our Mama encouraged us to visit her as often as possible.

Those were lonely days for our grandmother, and you could sure tell it when you walked into her small apartment. Mamaw would be sitting in a comfortable chair, in a pretty dress, looking out the window. Her long hair would be up in a tight, French-twist on the back of her head. Our conversation went something like this: 'Hi, Mamaw,' I would say with a smile. 'Oh, hello,' she would answer softly, always a little surprised to have a visitor. After our greetings, there was little more to talk about, and now I wish I had thought of the idea to read aloud to her. Back in the early 1960s, just after her husband had passed away, our grandmother lived in a children's home, in

Hapeville, Georgia, serving as a piano teacher for all of the children.

> "The truth is, once you learn how to die, you learn how to live."
>
> *Morrie Schwartz to Mitch in*
> *Tuesdays With Morrie*

She loved journaling, reading, and all sorts of things. Reading aloud to her would've given us interesting things to talk about.

My Daddy and I played a game during our visits in his last years. A trivia game of sorts. I would name some historical event, or a famous person and Daddy would tell me everything he knew about the subject. Then, I would take out my I-phone and google the topic at hand. We would soon see how his knowledge lined up with our findings. Daddy was always amazed at how quick I pulled the information up on my pocket-sized phone, and I was stunned with how 'spot-on' he was with his facts. Living until age 93, this kept us engaged when we were together.

Recently, I came up with the idea to read aloud to my husband's father, Don Page. We are about half way through one of my all-time favorite books: Tuesdays With Morrie, by, Mitch Albom, and we try to read together on Tuesdays in honor of Morrie Schwartz.

I mentioned this life-changing book in an earlier post when I wrote about Oseola McCarty.

March 14, 2016 marked one year since we moved Donny's father by ambulance from their hometown of Thomaston, Georgia so that we could keep a closer eye on him here near our home.

> "Life is a series of pulls back and forth... A tension of opposites, like a pull on a rubber band. Most of us live somewhere in the middle. A wrestling match...which side wins? Love wins. Love always wins."
>
> *Morrie Schwartz to Mitch in*
> *Tuesdays With Morrie*

Undergoing treatment for double pneumonia, Dad was immediately placed on a ventilator, which we were thankfully able to wean him off of within a few weeks. Saying these past 14 months have been tumultuous is an understatement. Dad has been in and out of the hospital too many times to count, rehabilitation for physical weakness, and he celebrated his 85th back on October 13, 2015. Today, even though he remains under the care of Hospice, and still gets confused about things, he is correctly working word puzzles in the newspaper. He is walking with the aid of a rollater, a rolling walker.

Christmas 2016 with Dad Page, Day Break Village, Kennesaw, Georgia.

Dad Page and his neighbor across the hall, Bob have been enjoying the story of Morrie Schwartz. We have laughed a lot and the reading has triggered many good memories from both gentlemen who are living out their last season of life. The next book I plan to share with them is The Last Lecture, by, Randy Pausch.

Is there someone in your path who might enjoy some one-on-one time with you?

It might be a small child or someone like Dad Page or my Mamaw.

Elementary age children and teens can read to their grandparents.

Reading together will make the world a better place.

Consider reading aloud one of your favorite stories!

Yes, letters and books can bring family members closer together and can even be a bridge of communication as you read the same book as your partner.

Read and share about what you have read!

This is just one idea on ways to nurture our spouses more and more with each passing day.

"So it's not gonna be easy. It's going to be really hard; we're gonna have to work at this every day, but I want to do that because I want you. I want all of you, forever, every day. You and me…everyday."

Nicholas Sparks, *The Notebook*

"Have nothing in your home that you do not know to be useful or believe to be beautiful."

William Morris

"There's an opportune time to do things, a right time for everything on the earth."

Ecclesiastes 3:1, The Message

Lesson 7

Nurture and Love Your Partner

As I shared before, Mama and Daddy had just celebrated their fifty-eighth wedding anniversary when Mama had her home-going on October 24, 2006. One conviction we six were given by Mama was to love, cherish, and nurture our partners. This is evidenced by the full devotion we six and our spouses have had for each other, some for more than four decades. All six of us are faithfully married to our first spouse, and our Mama loved our spouses, Jeanie, Jim, Jim, Rhys, Donny, and Lisa so well. As more were added to our family, Mama would forever bring to our minds one of her favorite quotes:

> "Love never divides, it only multiplies."
>
> Polly Walker

Mama and Daddy's Wedding Day, October 21, 1948.

During the last weeks of Mama's life, a steady flow of family members came by their apartment in Cartersville, Georgia.

I know I can speak for all that the example of our parents' marriage set us up for a successful path with our own partners. Marriage is challenging, and Mama would be the first to admit that marriage is never easy; in fact, she told us often that it was something she and her Johnny worked at every day. My sis, Kathy, reminded me that Mom would additionally tell us, "Now, I met your dad before I met any of you, and he will always come first in my book!" And he did! This served Kathy well as she and Jim went on to have six children and, now, seven grandchildren of their own.

A fisherman and musician, Daddy was happiest outdoors, playing his clarinet, and spending time with his family. Mama knew this about him, so she made sure time was allotted for these activities.

The A-framed home they purchased near Callaway Gardens in Pine Mountain, Georgia, featured a lake right outside their front door. This refuge rendered respite from their busy days in Decatur. While Daddy fished, Mama would read or journal, and just take in the natural setting.

From Mama's Journal

October 24, 1981

The weather is cool and rainy—I really don't mind, but it is hard for Johnny to fish. He caught one last night and one today. We went to the country store and then to the grocery store. The fish we cleaned and cooked was very good, so fresh. I have been resting and reading all weekend.

October 25, 1981

"The time has changed so we have an extra hour this weekend. After breakfast, Johnny went over for a paper, and now, he is fishing again. I am listening to Dr. Nelson Price @ Roswell Street Baptist Church. He is speaking on the full armor of God. Ephesians 6.

From Joan's Journal

Tuesday, January 1, 2013

Today is the first day of a new year! It is 9:00 p.m. and DP is already sleeping soundly beside me in bed. CHEERS to a New Year! I hope he knows how very thankful I am for him in my life. I feel I have a critical spirit towards him more than I should, certainly more than I want to! This is one thing I hope to work on in 2013. I love my husband, my best friend, and never, ever want to take him for granted.

As I have sat here and read some of James, I realize more than ever how impossible my every-day life is without my God in control. (especial-ly...w/o my allowing God to be in control) He is always ready and willing, but He is also very much a gentleman. I know He wants marriages to stay strong and He will help me with being less critical towards Donny in the days ahead.

Working just a few miles away, on Winn Way, near DeKalb General Hospital, Daddy would come home for lunch each day. Mama often quipped, "I married you for better, for worse, but not for lunch!" Still each weekday, Dad would sit at our table, munching on a sandwich, some Jell-O, and something small for dessert. Soon, he would be on his way back to the office, and Mama would continue on with her day.

Every single Thursday morning without fail, Mom would have her hair done and her sweetheart would arrive by noon to pick her up, take her to lunch, and then to an afternoon matinee, a movie of her choice. These weekly dates helped keep their marriage afloat when times were tough.

And times definitely got tough. In the late sixties, when I was a girl of ten, their oldest son, John Wade, would be drafted into Vietnam, and though he thankfully, survived, they would watch many young men come home severely injured, or worse, in body bags. Two families we were very close to soon mourned the loss of their boys, Mike Allen and Tim Faust. Never forgotten, we still search for their names whenever we have a chance to walk along The Vietnam Veterans Memorial Wall, etching their names on scraps of paper.

In addition to their weekly dates on Thursdays, they spent time together. T-I-M-E. There were, of course, no computers, no smart phones, less distractions than we have in our lives today. John Wade recalls Mama saying that some of her happiest moments were the early years that she and our father spent as missionaries in Africa. In any event, they were intentional about spending time together, and all the while, they taught us to do the same. And speaking of intentional, Mama was intentional about a slew of things, in addition to loving her man: practicing her faith by daily living it out, loving each one of us equally, loving her friends, loving, and continually feeding, lol, our long-haired teen friends without judgment and more.

Mama was "authentic" before that word became a buzz word!

Mama's influence and positivity was wide-spread, and her example of nurturing her Johnny was one way she impacted so many. She loved her husband with all of her heart, always supporting and caring for him. The benefits of following this loving example are truly timeless.

How can you and I follow this exemplary blueprint for loving and supporting our life partners?

Another prime example of love and devotion to a spouse was shared with me by my longtime friend, Sandy Gillam. You see, Sandy worked in Atlanta, Georgia, as a frontline Registered Nurse during the COVID-19 Pandemic. As we know, many patients were hospitalized without their loved ones there to serve as their advocates. Thankfully, Sandy kept a detailed journal of her challenging experiences and shares an entry with us here:

April 25, 2020

Covid Pandemic Observations

Yesterday, I worked on the Covid Unit 35W. I only had one patient who they were expecting to pass. He was 73 years of age, co-morbidities included seizure disorder, TBI after a motorcycle 3 years earlier, dementia, and Parkinson's Disease. He was unresponsive. To go into the Covid rooms, we have to put on a N-95 mask, a face shield, gown and gloves. I wanted to make sure he was clean, so I gave him a bath after my initial assessment. His wife (no one is allowed visitors) asked that we take the I-pad in and FaceTime with her. In case it was the last time she got to see him.

It was interesting, the 23rd Psalm was highlighted to me this past week. I thought about the valley of the shadow of death. I had the opportunity, the privilege of spending time with this patient as he went from this world. I got to pray for him, hold his hand, and make sure he heard his beloved wife's voice.

About five minutes before he passed, his wife told him he'd been a good husband, that he was the love of her life, and that she would always love him. He briefly opened his eyes and although he wasn't able to talk, he mouthed that he loved her. It was such a sweet, sacred, and heartbreaking moment. Then he passed @ 1645 as his wife, the love of his life, got to be with him.

Spend as much time with your partner as you can. Make all the memories possible. Here we are hiking in Switzerland in July

2018. The Matterhorn, certainly the most famous mountain in Europe—looms over the breathtaking Alpine panorama.

Family Pyramid. Hilton Head, South Carolina, 2013.

A Related Blog Post

October 2, 2020

Musings On Marriage
13,870 Days Since We Said "I Do"

Thanks to our long-time friend, Keith West, we met on a blind date on October 7, 1978 for a University of Georgia home football game.

On October 2, 2020, my husband, Donny and I celebrate 38 years of marriage.

The Dawgs conquered Ole Miss that day, in 1978, with a score of 42-3. What an awesome omen, a sign of good things to come regarding our future together.

We all know that a successful marriage doesn't just happen. There's no denying that this is a frightening time for couples. More than half of all first marriages end in divorce; 60 percent of second marriages fail.

Today, I have for you some musings on marriage, 13,505 days since we said "I Do".

- Marriage is hard work. This relationship is not for the faint of heart, but the rewards are great.
- You cannot change your spouse. Don't even try! "The greatest roadblock to a great relationship is trying to force a change through bribes or threats." Jonathan Lockwood Huie
- Keep your dreams alive together. "A dream you dream alone is only a dream. A dream you dream together becomes a reality." John Lennon
- Respect and love your spouse! A good, strong marriage is based on respect.
- Don't keep secrets from your spouse. "The fewer secrets you have, the happier you will be." Jonathan Lockwood Huie
- Give your spouse attention. "Gift the love of your life with a hold on social media, undistracted, untelevisioned,

unhurried attentiveness." Mary Anne Radmacher

- "...do not let the sun set upon your anger." Ephesians 4:26 "Make sure you never, never argue at night. You just lose a good night's sleep, and you can't settle anything until morning anyway." Rose Kennedy

- Arguing and disagreeing is perfectly normal in a good marriage and fusses make the reunion so much sweeter. I believe we grow in our relationships by reconciling our differences. That's how we become more loving people and truly experience the fruits of marriage.

- No one deserves unfaithfulness in a marriage! If a person is not happy enough to be faithful to the chosen one, one would hope they would just be honest and make their unhappiness known instead of sneaking around with another.

- Each spouse should have the room and freedom to be who they are as an individual. "Love allows your beloved the freedom to be unlike you. Attachment asks for conformity to your needs and desires." Deepak Chopra

- No one, absolutely no one should be verbally or physically abused in a marriage relationship. Take a firm stand against this kind of treatment. We teach people how to treat us.

- If this appeals to you and your love, take occasional, brief trips away from one another. Absence really does make the heart grow fonder. We've been doing this since the beginning of our 35 year marriage and believe it to be a great thing.

- When choosing a guy, take note of how he treats his mother. This may be a good sign about how he treats women, in general.
- Develop true love and an alignment of the same fundamental values in going for a successful marriage. "…a cord of three strands is not easily broken." Ecclesiastes 4:12
- At all costs, avoid criticizing your spouse, especially in the presence of others. It NEVER helps, and often makes things worse.
- Listen To Each Other. "No man is truly married until he understands every word his wife is not saying." Anonymous
- CARE deeply for your spouse. "Remember that children, marriages, and flower gardens reflect the kind of care they get." H. Jackson Brown, Jr.
- Share and grow a common faith. "Faith is the highest passion in a human being." Soren Kierkegaard "A cord of three strands is not easily broken." Ecclesiastes 4:12.
- Persistence always pays off! "Don't give up. There are too many naysayers out there who will try to discourage you. Don't listen to them. The only one who can make you give up is yourself." Sidney Sheldon "Many of life's failures are people who did not realize

how close they were to success when they gave up." Thomas Edison

- No matter who the bread-winner is, share the chores in the home and the care of the children. This builds both teamwork and camaraderie. "Many hands make light work." A Proverb

- A good marriage is an intimate and loving relationship which gives both partners security, friendship, companionship, support, comfort, and deep love that penetrates every aspect of life. None of this can be achieved without work and sacrifice.

- For a marriage to succeed, both partners must be committed to its success. Marriage is one of God's greatest gifts to humanity. It is the mystery of living as one flesh with another human being (Ephesians 5:31-32). Henry Cloud; John Townsend, Boundaries in Marriage

- Once your children are married, try your best not to give unsolicited advice. And if they do ask for advice, help them with that one thing, without bringing the subject up again. (unless they do)

- Look Around. Who are the ones you hang out with most of the time? Be sure they are folks who are as committed to a long-time marriage as you are.

- Say "I Love You", when you say "Good Night".

- Now that we are first-time grandparents, we are relishing this amazing season together. Supporting each other's efforts as we hold these tiny ones, care for them, and pour our hearts and souls into loving them.

- And another great tip added by my friend, Jan Kelly: Practice good manners with your spouse: please, thank you, excuse me, I'M SORRY (often!) Forgive Every Day. (thanks, Jan!)

What are some of your thoughts on how to build a successful marriage?

Soon after our second child, Walker, was born in 1992, I purchased a wooden placard that set forth this message:

"FIRST WE HAD EACH OTHER.
THEN WE HAD OUR KIDS.
NOW WE HAVE EVERYTHING."

The only thing I would add to this signpost is "then we had our kids AND grandkids," but of course, when I purchased this sign, I had no clue about the immense joy Tripp and Elizabeth would bring to our days. Growing up as number five of six children, it was easy to see that Mama wanted her kids to not only have roots, but she wanted each of us to confidently fly with free wings when the time came.

Let's carry on, as we see how Mama naturally gave us both roots and wings.

"Train up a child in the way he should go, and
when he is old, he will not depart from it."

Proverbs 22:6

"Let my teaching fall on you like rain; let my speech
settle like dew. Let my words fall like rain on tender
grass, like gentle showers on young plants. I will proclaim
the name of the Lord; how glorious is our God!"

Deuteronomy 32:2–3

Lesson 8

Give Your Children Roots and Wings

I t's been said that a mother raises her children to let them go.

> "Children are wet cement.
> Make the right impression in their lives."
>
> Anne Ortlund

Joan with Mama as she holds Amy, her first granddaughter, 1980.

The image of Mama in the morning is clear in my mind and heart. Her full-length, two-toned, velveteen robe with zipper down the front, colors of hot pink with a pale pink accent. Comfy slippers on her feet. On chilly mornings, the oven would be left slightly opened so that she could warm herself as she got breakfast going. With a mug of hot coffee nearby, she would rub her eyes sleepily. With a long wooden spoon, she would stir a huge pressure cooker filled with nutritious oatmeal. Cinnamon buttered toast would likely be served on the side with small glasses of orange juice. As I have grown up in this world, I have thought a lot about hungry children. Our frig and freezer were always packed. My family, thankfully, never experienced hunger, deprivation of food. Our parents spent four years in the heart of Africa before my birth. There, I am certain they witnessed this reality of not having enough provisions for the local families.

My first year as a teacher, Avondale Elementary School, DeKalb County, Georgia. Fifth grade, 1980–1981. I loved these students so much!

I saw it for myself as a schoolteacher at Avondale Elementary in the state of Georgia, beginning in 1980. Some of my students came to me from impoverished families. When we see difficult circumstances with our own hearts and minds, we are changed. Though I have never been in want, my heart has been made soft by my Mama to always consider those around me who might be in need. I have come to believe that this is an important piece of nurturing our offspring. No matter our income or socioeconomic status, all children will benefit by learning that there are families who are more well off than they are. And families who are less well off than they are. Along with this, children must be taught to have gratitude, especially during the formative years. When we were raising up Leah and Walker, I read a book by Anne Ortlund, titled *Children Are Wet Cement: Make the Right Impression On Their Lives*. A very useful book, I always loved this title. It reminded me of how impressionable our littles are. It is up to us to make the right impression on them, to model strong character for them, to love them without condition, just like Jesus loves us. That is what my Mama did as she nurtured us, giving us roots and wings to carry us throughout our lifetime.

Walker's High School Grad Party, May 2010 with his GoodDaddy,
my Daddy who passed on November 11, 2013. I am so
thankful for the roots my parents planted in our children.

Becoming an orphan as a small toddler, I wonder when Mama began to recognize the significance of building roots and wings within the hearts of her six children? Was it as a little girl adopted into the secure, godly Shivers family? Was it in the remote bush of Africa, as a twenty-three-year-old wife and mother, chasing after an independent only child? When did Mama discover the importance of the example she set for those before her?

Deuteronomy, the fifth book of the Jewish Torah, reminds us of the significance of building a faith foundation within our children as they grow.

Remember God's Words:

> Teach them to your children, speaking about them when you sit at home and when you walk along the road, when you lie down and when you get up. Write them on the doorposts of your houses and gates, so that as long as the heavens are above the earth, your days and those of your children may be multiplied in the land that the LORD swore to give your fathers...

> Deuteronomy 11:19–21

Mama planted roots of compassion into each one of us. I'll never forget the summer I was eleven years old, going on twelve; 1970. After watching the Jerry Lewis Telethons through the years, I decided I wanted to create and host a carnival to benefit "Jerry's Kids." The Muscular Dystrophy Carnival kit came in the mail and included tickets, posters and a detailed idea pamphlet to help us raise the funds to find a cure for the disease. Our family had watched hours of the Jerry Lewis Telethons through the years, and I wanted to do my part to help the kids we saw in the images on our black and white TV. Our backyard was perfect for this kind of thing, and I am sure I recruited Laura and Billy to help me out. I have no doubt that when Mama heard my idea, it sounded like a lot of work. That said, she never discouraged me from doing something that would help out another person. I remember excitedly waiting for my kit to arrive in the mail! We had bobbing for apples and the floating duck game, where you picked a duck and got a prize based on the number on the bottom of the duck. There were magic shows, fortune-telling booths, Kool-Aid and brownie stands. Everything required a ticket and the tickets cost a nickel each. Kids came from our church, our school, Fernbank Elementary, and surrounding streets after seeing our posterboards nailed to wooden telephone poles. Borrowed card tables for stations were set up in a big horseshoe around our backyard. There was Kool-Aid to be mixed up, cookies and brownies to be baked, and divided into baggies. All of our neighbors were invited, and we had quite an enormous crowd. I don't recall how much money was raised, likely less than $200, including some generous donations. I can, however, easily reminisce about how proud I felt for helping out Jerry's kids who had muscular dystrophy. This backyard carnival helped to instill in me a lifetime compassion for helping others.

Walker takes his first step with GoodMama's help. 1993.

LESSON 8

The following poem was pulled from a small book gifted to Mary Ann and Jim on their first wedding anniversary, August 25, 1974. The gift was from Jim and Kathy who were married two years later in 1975.

TEACHER OF LOVE

My mother taught me love; the love of high
The constant, changeless love of earth and sky,
The love of singing words, the love of plain
Sincerity and truth in act and thought,
The love of service and helpfulness,
The love of honest work, securely wrought,
And fortitude undaunted by distress.
My mother taught deep, lasting love to me
Of all things good and beautiful, with no
Great need of words, since love and bravery
And beauty and integrity are so
Much part of all her life and character
I learned the love of them in loving her.
From 'The Greatest of These...'
Jane Merchant

Walker and his GoodMama, January 1993.

Some close family friends have recently decided to be foster parents. All children need roots and wings. Foster kids, adopted kids, birth kids, grandkids, neighborhood kids. Yes, all kids need nurturing, love, security. How can you and I be a part of instilling roots and wings into a child today?

Related Blog Post

June 1, 2015

Grandparenting & Parenting: 4 Ways To Plant Roots and Strengthen Wings This Summer

Always knowing I wanted to be a mother, when I was an "aunt", not yet a Mommy, I loved hanging out with my nieces and nephews whenever I could. Guess I wanted to practice being a Mom. I wrote this out in calligraphy for my sisters to have in their homes, long before we had children of our own:

"We give our children two things. The first is roots, the second is wings."

I believe this brief statement is parenting in a nutshell.

I recently ran across this poem that I had never heard before on this very thing:

Roots and Wings
By, Denis Waitley

If I had two wishes, I know what they would be
I'd wish for roots to cling to, and wings to set me
    free.
Roots of inner values, like rings within a tree,
And wings of independence to seek my destiny.
Roots to hold forever to keep me safe and strong,
To let me know you love me when I've done
    something wrong.
To show me by example, and help me learn to
    choose
To take those actions every day to win instead of
    lose.
Just be there when I need you, to tell me it's
    alright
To face my fear of falling when I test my wings
    in flight.
Don't make my life too easy, it's better if I try;
And fail and get back up myself, so I can learn
    to fly.
If I had two wishes, and two were all I had,
And they could just be granted, by my Mama
    and my Dad;

I wouldn't ask for money or any store-bought
    things.
The greatest gifts I'd ask for are simply roots and
    wings.

In 2007, Leah was a senior in high school, and we were all itching for that next season. Those of you who have graduated high school seniors know what I am referring to. A little sad, with my firstborn preparing for takeoff, God gave me a visual I have never forgotten. A bird came into our home and flew into the highest corner of our ceiling. My friend, Beth Andersen, had just arrived for coffee and muffins. We were both trying to help the bird return safely to the familiar outdoors. We tried different strategies like waving a broom at it, opening windows and doors before we decided to just "let it be". Soon, the bird took leave on its own, spreading its wings and flying on out.

August 6, 2007
My Dearest Daughter, Leah,
"This is your time,
This is your Dance.
Leave NOTHING to chance!"
I cut these quotes from some of your
grad cards and made you a collage!
Hopefully, you can use this small plate
stand to prop it up somewhere in your
new home.
I love you, but then, you already know that.
I'll miss you, but then, you already know that, too!
OK, so what can I tell you that you
may not have thought of lately??
I know how determined you can be
when you set your mind on something, so set your sights
high in regards to your future.
Take time out to get to know the hearts of the friends you meet.
And always remember that GOD and YOU are your two
best friends. Talk to Him often and allow Him to direct your paths.
Always treat yourself well (positive self-talk, fitness, etc)
If your conscience is "talking to you" about something,
that very well could be the Holy Spirit, so LISTEN!
"IF IT IS TO BE, IT'S UP TO ME!"
Love,
MOMMY

This served as a solid reminder to me that we had done our best to give Leah deep roots, and it was now time for her to fly on out into a more independent world.

Four Ways to Plant Roots and Strengthen Roots in our Children:

(1) Foster Friendships-yours and theirs. Find like-minded Moms and share pool time, coffee time, play time with fellow Moms and children. Join with other families to take field trips to the Center for Puppetry Arts in Atlanta or Tellus Science Museum in Cartersville, Georgia.

Consider planning a MUST Summer Lunch Party joining families to help those in need.

(2) Capture Teachable Moments-Walk in the rain when there is no danger of lightning, talk about respecting nature and why it's important to not be a litter bug, model kindness to others you meet in your path with a smile and an encouraging word, talk to your children and explain anything that may come up in your moments...whether it be a homeless person or someone with a severe disability.

Go to your public library and just sit and read. Our children checked out the number of books which equaled their age. I believe values are more "caught than taught". Have a chore list and get your children involved in cooking and laundry as early as possible. And most of all, teach your children to pray with a grateful heart each day.

(3) Choose Your Battles-All children need boundaries, and though they would never admit it out loud, those boundaries which you provide help them to feel safe. As your children grow, there will be more and more discussions about things they want to do, and you will have the final say. Giving children choices will help them to build trust in their ability to make decisions. When Leah was around six years old, she was beginning to develop a ton of independence and it challenged me. One of our battles was what she wanted to wear to school-mismatched clothing, at times. I came up with a plan that worked well. I chose three outfits and placed them on her bed. Leah got to choose from the three outfits, and this gave her the independence she longed for. As discussions ("aka: arguments") come up, decide if it is really worth it to argue about or if it would be better to let that one go. Choosing your battles will relieve the stress of parenting. And remember, rebellion may happen in our children where there is a lack of relationship.

(4) Insist on an Afternoon Siesta-I got this one from my Mama. When the grandchildren would come to visit, she would enforce a one hour break each afternoon. No one *had* to "sleep", though I bet Mama did!

The Siesta Time could be for reading or doing something quietly in your room and everyone got a break from the busy, fun vacations at GoodMama and GoodDaddy's lake-front home in rural Mississippi. Try this in your own home. This habit will energize you, helping you to enjoy the remainder of the days even more.

How will you and I plant deep roots and strengthen wings in the lives of your children and grandchildren?

Twenty-three new little miracles have been laid in this amazing cradle designed with love by Augustus "Gus" Colquitt! I am thankful to my friends, Pendy and Trish for giving me plaques to keep track of all the babies.

The following babies slept in this handcrafted cradle:

EVERYONE IS THANKFUL FOR ME! Our two grands,
Tripp and Elizabeth born two weeks apart. Thanksgiving, 2018.
They are in a cradle created for Leah Suzanne Page in 1988.

> "He knew you before you were born…"
>
> Psalm 139

Leah Suzanne Page (October 8, 1988)
Marie Louise Corrigan (April 18, 1990)
Kevin Michael Seder (August 31, 1990)
Andrew Blaise Linter (April 26, 1991)
Donald Walker Page (February 27, 1992)
Brendan Nizar Oweida (July 20, 1992)
John Patrick Lintner (April 30, 1993)
William Thomas Kommor (August 9, 1993)
Cori Danielle Pinto (April 25, 1994)
Molly Kathryn West (January 12, 1995)
Stephen Patrick Oweida (October 26, 1995)
Liam Khory Oweida (April 24, 1998)
Garrett Keith West (July 27, 1993)
Jillian Claire Walker (February 18, 1999)
John Caleb Oweida (July 8, 2000)
William Jackson Linter (November 10, 2000)
Andrew Lee Galloway (August 6, 2001)
Charles Alexander Seder (July 21, 2002)
Caleb Thomas Galloway (October 3, 2003)
Kayla Marie Seder (January 11, 2005)
Jacob Edward Seder (August 11, 2006)
Michael Scott Andrews III (August 24, 2018)
Elizabeth Noel Page (September 7, 2018)

Thanksgiving 2018. Gratefulness for two three-month-old grandchildren.

When children are small, the hours are long, while the years are short.

Time is going by, no matter what, so decide today how to plant deep roots in the ones God has gifted you with.

Leah, age three, with her new little brother, Walker, six months, 1992.

How do you measure, measure a year?
In daylights, in sunsets, in midnights, in cups of coffee.
In inches, in miles, in laughter, in strife.
In 525,600 minutes.
How do you measure a year in the life?
How about love?
Measure in love.
(From the song "Seasons of Love," original Broadway show: *Rent*)

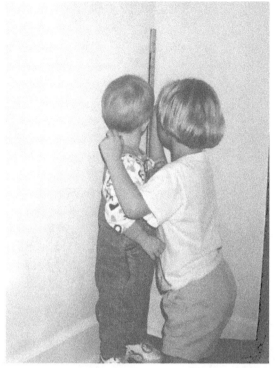

Big sis, Leah measures her little brother, Walker's height, 1993.

From Mama's Journal

October 11, 1985

It has been my belief since Shane, our first grandchild was born that we are given a second chance with grandchildren. These little children who have entered our lives give us a chance to teach them our basic beliefs and principals of God and Life. Which while as busy parents, we do not take the time. Last August, one beautiful afternoon, I really got that chance. Mary Ann called me and asked it I wanted to go to the beach. My answer was quick: "That sounds like a bit of heaven, when do we leave?" We had a good trip down stopping in Augusta to eat and to go to a farmer's market where we bought a watermelon for $.50 along with other good fruits and vegetables.,

Mary Ann, Amy, Ricky and Joan Davis were with us when we began to take our beach walk on Tuesday afternoon. The sun was going down and the breeze was wonderful on our faces.

Amy and I were leading the way and had picked up a few shells. I had some in my pocket. The tide was coming in and we started back up the beach towards our house. There was a small stream of tide water we needed to cross in order to shorten our way. Amy and I started across, the others stopped to see if we could make it across. The water came up to my knees and I could feel my feet beginning to sink. I had on some old sandals. Amy was holding my right hand. Also, in my right hand, I held a beautiful angel wing shell.

All of a sudden, I lost my balance and was down on my knees in the water. Of course, Amy's head went under. Mary Ann and our friend, Joan were laughing, as we were really in no danger. When I saw Amy's look of surprise, I started to laugh, too. The first thing that came to my tongue was to say to Amy that the angel wing had held us up. We laughed all the way home. I forgot how tired I was, even though my shoes were waterlogged, and my clothes were soaked.

The angel wing, which is very fragile, was not broken. This reminded me of what I tried to teach my own children. We only have to reach out and touch God's hand, and it is always there. We are told in the Bible-"Those that have faith in the Lord will rise up on eagle's wings," but I am thinking maybe angel wings are just as strong. We were unhurt in our fall. Amy was not afraid, just surprised.

As we returned to our house back down the beach, we were all wet, but happy. Again, I forgot how tired I was because I had a new small person to teach again. We sure enjoyed our trip to the beach. It was short, but soul-renewing. A time to pause and be still and listen to God as He talked with us.

From Joan's Journal

Wednesday, July 11, 1990

I took Leah to her MMO (Mom's Morning Out) program today. She didn't cry when I left (as she sometimes does) and the teachers said the usual things (music to a young mommy's ears): "She is so sweet." And "Leah plays so well." Knowing that she is a happy and secure baby makes me feel so good.

At 21 months, Leah is active! And she is independent, too! She doesn't really want to hold my hand, but she is learning that she will be safer around cars when she does. Even though we do want a second child someday, I am truly glad Leah is the only one for now. It is so much fun spending time with her! When God is ready, He will bless us with a brother or sister for Leah. Until then, I feel so lucky to have her in our home and in our life. Donny and I work hard taking care of her, but she gives us back so much more with her love and her laughter. We are taking a trip next week and we're thankful that Leah will be in such

good hands with her Uncle Rhys, Aunt Laura Lea
and her cousins, Brad and Pamela.

Another way Mama loved her children and grands was by sewing for them. Mama loved creating beautiful stamped cross stitch gifts for all. This included precious baby quilts for her grands and more. Here are two cherished pieces that are in our home today.

Nurturing our two children has been the greatest privilege in my life. Bringing a tiny new human being into this world and then trying to raise this little soul properly for the next eighteen years. As I have observed our two children as parents, along with their loving, supportive spouses, since 2018, I have watched their roots go deeper. Their wings have spread wider. Through thick and thin, we have traveled life together, and it has been so much fun! In fact, as my friend, Lynn's late father, Buz McGriff said often, "We have so much love and fun, we can wallow in it!"

As we've considered already, no matter what, tough times do come to all in the process of living. When adversity rolled in, Mama would inevitably remind us, "This, too, shall pass." While this common phrase has a long history, the origin cannot be pinned down to one person. This quote is a reminder for us all that regardless of how the happenstances of life unfold. And how it has dealt us its hand for us to play in life, *it will soon pass.*

Strenuous seasons come and go in this life. From the cradle to the coffin, affliction and sorrow are the appointed lot of humans. Souls come into the world with a wailing cry, and then often leave it with an agonizing groan.

I believe that's why Mama wanted to be sure we understood that circumstances do change over time. She wanted us to stop, take a breath, and recognize that demanding days would pass.

"When you come to the end of your rope, tie a knot and hang on."

Franklin D. Roosevelt

"Let perseverance be your engine and hope, your fuel."

H. Jackson Brown Jr.

"Seeds of faith are always within us; sometimes it takes
a crisis to nourish and encourage their growth."

Susan Taylor

"If you are going through hell, keep going."

Winston Churchill

"I am not afraid of storms, for I am learning how to sail my ship."

Louisa May Alcott

Lesson 9

This, Too, Shall Pass

Today's date is May 20, 2020. This means that our world as we once knew it has been turned upside down in the past four months or so. The COVID-19 global pandemic spread to the United States on January 19, 2020. Coronavirus (COVID-19) is a novel infectious disease caused by severe acute respiratory syndrome coronavirus. The first confirmed US cases of local transmission were recorded in January and the first known deaths happened in February. By the end of March, cases had occurred in all fifty US states, DC, and all inhabited US territories except American Samoa. As of May 13, 2020, the US has the most confirmed active cases and deaths in the world, and its death rate was 206 per million people, the tenth-highest rate globally. So many memories of this crazy, tumultuous timeframe are mulling thorough my mind. What memories stand out the most for you and your family as you reconsider the start of 2020?

Expressions we have rarely used in our lifetimes are now commonplace, like quarantine, unprecedented, and shelter-in-place. Birthday parties have been placed on hold. Funerals only allow a maximum of ten loved ones to gather to celebrate the life of a loved one. Hospitals allow no visitors, even the patient's immediate family are barred from entering. My best friends, Mary and Kelly, both RNs have been carrying crazy long hours! All front-line, essential workers have been busting it, working long, difficult hours. Shuffling our groceries for us. Putting themselves at risk while tending to the very sick patients. Ensuring that our trash is moved beyond our living space. Making sure our letters and bills arrive in our mailbox in a timely manner. And speaking of bills, the economic downturn has been likened to 2008. A plunging stock-market. The widening shadow of recession. Federal interest rate cuts and government stimulus.

For many Americans, the stomach-churning market dropping and growing recession talk of the past few weeks—triggered by the global spread of the coronavirus—are reviving memories of the 2008 financial crisis and Great Recession.

While the toll the infection ultimately takes on the nation isn't clear, many professionals are hopeful that the economic upheaval caused by the outbreak will likely not be nearly as damaging or long-lasting as the historic downturn of 2007–2009.

One of the pieces that has been the most difficult has been watching how this horrific pandemic has threatened the well-being of our senior citizens. A group that I am well aware of and I am close to joining. Having gone through the deaths of both of my parents, as well as both of Donny's, it is clear to me how very vulnerable this population is. I've been wondering what Mama would say if she was here today. I believe she would say, "This, too, shall pass. Let's wait and see what the morning brings."

This was a common response during times of emergencies, uncertainties, and flat-out, worrisome seasons. This, too, shall pass. Whether it was waiting to hear from John Wade while he served our country in a foreign land as a Marine, a serious illness that a family member was going through, or moving to a new area like Decatur, Georgia where her family knew no one, Mama felt confidently at peace that the difficult and uncertain season would pass.

> "Trust in the Lord with all your heart, and do not lean on your own understanding. In all your ways acknowledge him, and he will make your paths straight."
>
> Proverbs 3:5–6

From Mama's Journal

January 9, 1988

I went to bed about 8:00 p.m. and slept 'til 11. Got up and got some medicine for my hip and slept until 8:30 a.m. Will try to write some letters today.

Laura Lea called and said she and the children will come on January 29th for a week. They will travel on Amtrak.

January 29, 1988

We got up about 8:00 a.m. This is the day the children will arrive, and we are so excited! We ate lunch, then left for Hattiesburg. The train was on time and it was so good to see the children. Brad did not sleep on the train, Pamela slept about one hour. However, Laura was smiling and glad to see us. Brad went to sleep soon after we got on the country road. Pamela was restless. She finally came to sit with me. I am sure she was tired of her car seat. Soon, we fed the children, got them bathed and in bed. Then we talked and talked. Brad woke up at 5:30 (our time) and crawled into bed with us until Johnny built us a fire.

Later during the visit: This has been such a good visit, despite a lot of rain. We took Brad and Pamela to Bill's Dollar Store to get them some rain boots. Brad said, 'GoodMama, I am so glad you gave me these because I really do need them for fishing and for all this Mississippi mud.' He has been so cute. When he got locked out of his room and I opened it for him, he told Laura that he wanted to marry me. We've had such fun, and I am thankful I have been able to keep my hip pain away during their visit.

From Joan's Journal

Saturday, March 20, 2021

I keep thinking about my friend and neighbor, Sherri who passed away Wednesday night. I know she is well, in Glory, but what about those left behind? Her husband, her two grown children, their families. What about them? I know they will grieve. Duh! Age 62, my age, Sherri was called home and we are left here to miss her. To experience the absence, the void, her going on early leaves within each one of us. This morning, I was reading from one of my favorite devotions, Jesus Calling. I was reminded that "He showers us with blessings daily, but I sometimes do not perceive them. When my mind is stuck on a negative focus, I see neither Him nor his gifts. In faith, I want to thank Him for whatever is preoccupying my mind. Therefore, I can clear the blockage in order to find Him."

I wonder when Mama began to learn this lesson. Was it when she was a tot, close to the age of our grandchildren, Tripp and Elizabeth during COVID-19? As she was living in an orphanage? Did she learn patience earlier than the norm as she waited for her forever family?

Maybe it was later, in her early twenties as she boarded a ship for Brussels, Belgium, as a new wife and mommy. Polly and Johnny and their young son, John would travel to Belgium to brush up on their French language before heading south to the heart of Africa to serve as medical missionaries. Was this lesson learned aboard that ship as the disease of malaria would move from passenger to passenger. Mama and baby, John Wade quarantined themselves in their cramped cabin. Did she utter the words, a prayer of sorts, "This, too, shall pass," as she watched story after story of violent combat during the Vietnam War on our black and white television screen?

Another mantra Mama taught us was "Let's have guarded optimism." Whenever there were uncertain circumstances that involved waiting a brief or a long time, these four words somehow encouraged and comforted us in the situation.

And Mama often quipped, "Be careful what you pray for. And by no means should you ever pray for patience. Otherwise, God will surely give you a life circumstance to aid you in learning about patience."

Instead, Mama hoped and prayed for the courage to journey through her days until trying times passed. And somehow, they always did. In her sixties, while living the retired life in rural Mississippi, Mama seemed to suffer chronic hip issues and noted this in her journals. Seems she always knew the pain would pass.

The date was July 27, 2020, and Garrett Keith West's twenty-seventh birthday. A graduate student enrolled at SMU in, Garrett had been back with his folks in Marietta, GA, during COVID. He was continuing his studies remotely during the long, stretched-out days of the pandemic.

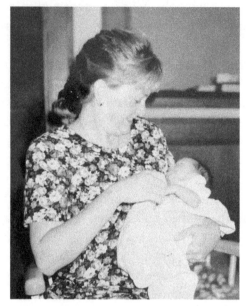

Karen and newborn, Garrett West, 1993.

Donny and I spontaneously jumped in the car and headed over to The Wests for a small birthday dinner. "Come Quick! WE have a surprise tonight!" Karen texted. As we showed up at their home, one of the first things we talked about is how crazy our world had been lately. A global pandemic? Who would have expected or predicted such a thing? Keith, per usual, greeted us with his positive, soft-spoken nature responding with this: "Yes, but this season has allowed for so much more family time, and besides that, this, too, shall pass." Keith had recently seen a sign with these four words on a long-distance bicycle ride. Placed clearly and visibly in a resident's front yard, the words had been imprinted in his mind.

Oh, and the exciting news in the West household? Via FaceTime, Kelsea, the West's first born announced from the Alexander home in Dallas, Texas, that she and Troy would be having a baby boy in early 2021. The Wests' first grandchild. We jumped up and down with excitement, as Molly, the West's youngest joined us from New York City. Donny and I were especially happy to welcome Keith and Karen to "The Club" of grandparenting. Surely the best club around.

THIS, TOO, SHALL PASS

A story by Pastor Andy Stanley

Sometimes I just want it to stop. Talk of COVID, looting, brutality. I lose my way. I become convinced that this "new normal" is real life. Then I meet an 87-year-old who talks of living through polio, diphtheria, Vietnam protests and yet is still enchanted with life.

He seemed surprised when I said that 2020 must be especially challenging for him. "No," he said slowly, looking me straight in the eyes. "I learned a long time ago to not see the world through the printed headlines, I see the world through the people that surround me. I see the world with the realization that we love big. Therefore, I just choose to write my own headlines:

"Husband loves wife today." "Family drops everything to come to Grandma's bedside." He patted my hand. "Old man makes new friend."

His words collide with my worries, freeing them from the tether I had been holding tight. They float away. I am left with a renewed spirit and a new way to write my own headlines.

Today is Friday, September 18, 2020. My sister, Laura Lea's birthday, though I am not with her to celebrate. I know she will have a super great day with her husband on Panama City Beach, just an hour west of me. You see, I am sitting here in Port St. Joe, Florida, grateful to Kay and Thomas Andrews, who loaned me their quaint Gulf Coast cottage for a writing retreat. I have been here alone all week thinking, writing, musing. Often called the Forgotten Coast, this community is nestled in the panhandle of the Sunshine State. When the weather is clear, my favorite thing to do is to drive their golf cart to the nearby Shipwreck Raw Bar. Picking up some fresh, boiled shrimp to go, I am soon on my way back to the solitude of the cottage. Floridians on the Panhandle, along with residents in neighboring coastal states will remember this past week as that time Hurricane Sally came to town. "Ride, Sally, ride" my friend, Kathy said in jest as she witnessed firsthand the storm crashing against her home. Richard and Kathy live in Pensacola Beach, Florida, and lost power for a long while. Thanks to a house-wide generator, The Owens were able to offer freezer space and a mug of hot coffee to the friends on their street. For me, away from the eye of Sally, there was day after day of torrential rains and high winds: a perfect climate for a writer. I knew from experience that the storm would pass. I hear in my mind's voice, "Honey, this, too, shall pass." Friends text me during the week while I am here alone. "Aren't you afraid?" they'd ask me with concern. I wasn't.

And today, we just returned from a bike ride, Donny arrived yesterday afternoon and brought the sunshine with him. This, too, shall pass. After a full week of rain, the sun has returned. Tomorrow, we will go on a day trip, visiting stunning Cape San Blas for our very first time. The storm has passed. We will enjoy the soft, white pristine beach of the Cape, an irresistible part of the state's Emerald coast. Yes, the sun is shining, and the storm has passed.

Thanksgiving 2020 will be here soon. We just received news that a dear friend has received difficult news without any warning. Life is like that sometimes, isn't it? Out of nowhere, we are blindsided with current events that were 100 percent unexpected. Advanced ovarian cancer. What? Advanced ovarian cancer, my friend repeated as he shared his wife's diagnosis with me. Married more than thirty years, our friends have a solid, strong partnership. Our friends are people of faith. They will battle back against this disease as a team, along with their three young adult children. We will be standing shoulder-to-shoulder with them as they fight. Our prayers will be for a reasonable treatment road, a route to remission. Please, Lord.

This, too, shall pass.

> "Weeping may endure for the night, but Joy comes in the morning."
>
> Psalm 30:5

Thank you, Lord, for your promise that this, too, shall pass.

When have you found yourself in difficult, adverse circumstances? A time that you were beginning to believe it would last forever. Let's always remember that with faith, prayer, and trust, burdensome times will surely pass.

A Related Blog Post

April 22, 2020

Pandemic Alterations
Let's Work Our Muscles!

Have you considered some alterations you would like to see in your life journey? Seriously, the vast majority of us have had extra time to consider our lives and our ways of living out our days. This reminds me of a favorite hit from the Broadway hit, RENT. Seasons Of Love. "525,600 minutes, 525,600 moments, how do you measure a year in a life? How do you measure a year? In daylights, in sunsets, in midnights, in cups of coffee, in inches, in miles, in laughter, in strife. In 525,600 minutes. How do you measure a year in a life. Measure your life in love."

It's easy to recall all the hype that came with the introduction of a brand, new decade just 113 days ago. 2020 had quite the ring to it didn't it!?! Now that the first quarter of this new year has sailed us by, we are left here wondering what has happened. That trio of months seems like a long time ago, doesn't it? It does to me! So much has changed.

This Global Pandemic has truly turned our world upside down, hasn't it? This unprecedented season came to us with very little notice and by mid-March, our schools and "non-essential" establishments were shutting down.

We were, in fact, blindsided when

COVID-19 came to town, weren't we!?

"In the rush to return to normal, use this time to consider which parts of normal are actually worth rushing back to." David Hollis

How have you and I navigated this new normal? Have you, like me, had more pajama pants…yoga pants…in the laundry basket than ever before? More food in the fridge, the pantry than ever before? More rest and relaxation than ever before? More time to think, to reflect than ever before? If so, then WE are the lucky ones. Unlike the countless first responders who are carrying forty, fifty, sixty-plus hours on the front line, quarantining from their families, literally laying their lives on the lines for the rest of us.

Yes, we are the lucky ones if we have the resources, shelter, and food that we all need. WE are especially fortunate if we have a stable foundation of love and emotional support under our roofs, as well.

How is our overall mental health?

I recently read a devotion that reminds me that life takes muscle work and resilience. I want to be willing to make changes as life evolves.

Otherwise, I am just "a bystander." And I don't know about you, but I want to be "a participant" in this life, not just someone who is here and accounted for, but not really taking part, not connecting, not interacting, not having an impact.

I am learning that the best way to bring peace to my external circumstances is to begin with internal work. Internal peace will begin to settle external chaos.

Here is an excerpt from the devo I read:

"I'm convinced that life without risk isn't much of a life. There's a certain comfort in predict-ability. But it's the kind of comfort you don't find when you're moving and growing. It's the comfort you find in hibernation.

If you've followed sports or been around ath-letes, you know that an athlete regularly stretches his muscles to the point where they burn. Otherwise, these muscles become inflexible, unresponsive, and easily fatigued. The same is true with your soul. It must be regularly stretched. Failure to do so gives you comfort in the short-term, but ultimately leaves you emotionally and spiritually unfit.

Connecting, loving, and pursuing dreams, all require risk and energy! Yes, you'll be stretched to the point of discomfort. Yes, you may experience some hurt and disappointment. But these are far better alternatives than the loneliness, boredom, and quiet desperation that accompany a life without risk."

~Steve Arterburn, New Life Live~

While it is not always comfortable, I want to stretch ALL of my muscles from here on out! My physical muscles, my faith muscles, my brain muscles, my compassion for others' muscles. ALL of these, and more.

In addition, I want to discover what in my life is no longer serving me well.

Maybe it's a bad habit I have been carrying around for some time. A routine that has become commonplace. A Rut. A pattern that is no longer useful. A temperament that is not as kind as I would like. Did you know? A rut can turn into a six-foot grave if we keep digging. The only difference between a rut and a grave is the depth of the hole and how long you plan to stay in it. If you and I are in a rut right now, the answer to getting out is taking action.

There is no better time than a pandemic to make the changes we want to make, when many of us are allotted an extra span of time to ponder this.

If only we will.

What is it for you and for me that we would like to change and alter for the days ahead as we all begin to live our "new normal"? What pandemic alterations would we like to create?

What is no longer serving us?

Yes, it can be difficult, and risky, too. But, so, so worth it. It is truly a Fork in the Road, and we get to choose the way.

Let's Start Today!

How do we continue moving forward while waiting for a challenging time to pass? We stay calm and we carry on. We smile even when we don't feel like it.

A smile can be contagious within our family units and groups of friends.

A smile can download positivity in the midst of distress.

A smile can bring warmth to an otherwise cool environment.

A smile can initiate an encouraging thought when encountering someone who is down.

A smile can change another's day in the blink of an eye.

A smile can speak volumes when there are no words.

A smile is a facelift everyone can afford.

"Too often we underestimate the power of a touch, a smile, a kind word, a listening ear, an honest compliment, or the smallest act of caring, all of which have the potential to turn a life around."

Leo Buscaglia

"Every time you smile at someone, it is an action of love, a gift to that person, a beautiful thing."

Mother Teresa

Lesson 10

Smile

Smiling reminds me of a song from my childhood: *"I've got that joy, joy, joy, joy down in my heart... ♪♫♫."* Once that song gets into your mind, you will be singing it all day! True joy can be attained as part of the fruit of the Spirit, as in Galatians 5:22.

> *But what happens when we live God's way? He brings gifts into our lives, much the same way that fruit appears in an orchard—things like affection for others, exuberance about life, serenity. We develop a willingness to stick with things, a sense of compassion in the heart, and a conviction that a basic holiness permeates things and people. We find ourselves involved in loyal commitments, not needing to force our way in life, able to marshal and direct our energies wisely.*
>
> Galatians 5:22–23, The Message

It is that overwhelming sense of comfort and contentment that floods one's soul.

Ten years of retirement in rural Mississippi brought smiles to us all. Silver Run Lake. In a lake front, A-frame home, our mom and dad welcomed their grown children's families again and again. They loved welcoming others, both family and friends.

Anne Page visits with Mom and Dad in Silver Run, Mississippi.

In 1992, Leah, Walker and Joan travel to Mississippi on Amtrak to visit with GoodMama and GoodDaddy.

The kind of feeling that makes you want to smile. My Mama always had a ready smile, the kind that forms naturally without much effort. Mama held a strong conviction that no matter how tough life could seem on a given day, she could always find a reason to smile, and she taught the six of us to do the same.

I honestly do not know if Mama realized that a gentle smile could provide so many positive gains, however there is no doubt that the following benefits certainly showed up in her everyday life: Neurotransmitters called endorphins are released when you smile. Endorphins make us feel happier and less stressed. While the release of endorphins is increased, the stress hormone cortisol is reduced. Laughing expands the lungs, stretches the muscles in the body and stimulates homeostasis. A good laugh can be an effective way to release emotions. Now, doesn't that list make you want to smile more!?

Mama and Daddy served as medical missionaries for five years in Belgian Congo during the early 1950s. There was definitely a language barrier between the two of them and the natives who lived there. Body language and smiles became more important than ever during those five years.

2003, Rio de Janeiro on my first trip there. I met these brothers in the clinic. The older one followed me around all day, waiting for another hug.

Everyone smiles in the same language. Values are caught more than taught. With the language barrier on international mission trips, I utilized a ready smile often. When our niece, Amy Elrod Fairchild, lived and served in Rio de Janeiro, Brazil, I had the chance to serve there with her for more than a half dozen times in the early 2000s. It was pure joy joining her teams so many times. A fluent speaker of the Portuguese language and a nurse, Amy inspired me again and again in her encounters with the gracious Brazilians. I will be forever indebted to my niece, Amy Elrod Fairchild, her parents, team leaders; Mary Ann and Jim, team leaders; Sharon and Ray Fairchild; and all the incredibly gifted intrepreters who served with us on every trip. These life-changing mission trips would have been impossible without our interpreters, Mirian Santana Eloy (pictured here with me) Tiago Silva (my very first interpreter in 2003), Andre Nobrega, Gus Foster, Norma Baldner Moraes, Louise Marques, and so, so many gifted others.

On my first visit, in 2003, I will always remember a young boy of about nine years of age following me around for the entire day after I offered him a smile and a band-aid for a small cut. We never exchanged a word because of our language barrier, but there was certainly no obstacle sitting between our hearts. Our frequent hugs as he followed me around were warm.

We have all heard that a smile has been described as having the power to light up a room. While it is positively a beautiful sentiment, it also carries more than a hint of truth. A warm and genuine smile can be the very thing that helps an uncertain person feel more comfortable in an unfamiliar setting. That same smile can change someone's entire bad day around.

There is no surprise that a more severe or negative facial expression like frowns, scowls, and grimaces actually work in the opposite manner, effectively pushing people away. Instead, a genuine smile can draw people in. That is what our Mama did.

Mama was always drawing others in.

Mama drew people in wherever she went. It was with her sensitive responses and her ready smile that she captured the interest of others into herself. Mama's loving heart always had room to hold one more soul.

I attended a wonderful garden party wedding shower last week for our friend, Sara's son's bride, Caroline. As I sat in the spring sunshine with the grandmother of the groom, Jane Hamby, I was so moved by a story she shared. "You know, I just love people. We never know what we will miss by not taking the chance to reach out to others who are in our path; engaging with them."

Sara's Momma continued, "When our son, Jay passed last December 11, 2020, at the age of sixty-four, instead of saying 'I am so sorry,' a friend said, 'Tell me about your Jay.'"

Have you heard the phrase, "A smile is a frown turned upside down."?

March 2017 Breckenridge, with our two awesome
"in-law" kids, Jessica and Scott.

Did you know?

It requires more facial muscles to frown than to smile. If you
are not in the habit of having a ready smile, like my Mama, practice
in the mirror. I know this sounds silly, but in my sister, Laura Lea's
opinion, this isn't foolish at all! You see, following the passing of her
son, Brad, in April 2009, Laura found herself having to "practice"
smiling again. I cannot personally attest to how the loss of a child
feels, even though I have walked closely beside my sis during her grief
journey. As time went by, Laura shared with me that she would literally practice smiling at their dog, Luke, and in her bathroom mirror.
Smiling did not come naturally for a terribly long time after Brad's

passing…yet Laura Lea knew from our dear Mama's lessons, that a ready smile held many advantages to a healthy, well-rounded life.

From Mama's Journal

March 29, 2004

SEDER Wedding Anniversary, 1975. Called Kathy. Mailed birthday package to Billy-44th. Gus Colquitt passed away.

Funeral in Yatesville, Georgia 11:00 a.m. on March 31.

'You have been on my mind so much lately, and today a certain memory of you warmed my heart and made me smile."

From Joan's Journal

Saturday, February 26, 2011

I have to journal! I am thankful I have the time. It is 4:40 p.m., a beautiful spring-like day, high sixties, blue sky. My heart is so happy. Walker will be 19 tomorrow, celebrating as a freshman at Wheaton College, 700 miles away from our home. A special memory from today forever for me will be reading aloud my 1992 journal to Donny as we recalled the events of his birth. This definitely brought smiles to us both. Yesterday, Ev (from Estes Park, Colorado) sent all of us FFs a neat saying about how important girlfriends are in our lives and how spending time together feeds our brains serotonin. That is a true and awesome thought!

But how do we smile behind a mask? During this global pandemic that began in late 2019 and early 2020 has caused me to think a lot about how important it is to smile with our eyes. Did you know? Matthew 6:22 reminds us that our eyes are the windows to our soul. Smiling with your eyes is hard to fake. It helps to channel good thoughts, so you'll be genuine and sincere. Once you get really good at it, you can even smile using only your eyes! This reminds me of the importance of encouraging those in our paths, whether it be with a smile, word, or deed.

I love this old story about a group of frogs, and it goes like this:

> *The group of frogs were traveling through the woods and two of them fell into a deep pit. When the other frogs saw how deep the pit was, they told the two frogs that they were as good as dead. The two frogs ignored their comments and tried to jump out of the pit with all of their might. The other frogs kept telling them to stop, that they were as good as dead. Finally, one of the frogs took heed to what the other frogs were saying and gave up. He fell down and died. The other frog continued to jump as hard as he could. Once again, the crowd of frogs yelled at him to stop the pain and just die. He jumped even harder, and finally made it out. When he got out, the other frogs said, "Did you not hear us?" The frog explained to them that he was deaf. He thought they were encouraging him the entire time.*

Moral of the frog story: There is power of life and death in the tongue. An encouraging word (or smile!) to someone who is down can lift them up and help them make it through the day. So let's be careful of what we say and how we treat those in our path. Let's speak life to those we pass in our days. The power of a smile…it cannot be underestimated. The impact of a ready smile, just like my Mama.

There is a group of friends that make me smile every time I think of them. We call ourselves Forever Friends. Since the early 1960s anyway, so nearly forever. Cindy, Jan, Lynn, Jane Ellen, Debbie, Mary, Evelyn, and me. The eight of us make up The FFs.

We grew up in Decatur, Georgia, attending Fernbank Elementary and Druid Hills High School together. They may not know this, but these girlfriends are the planets in my personal solar system. I know myself better because I know them. We live in four different states. Even when I don't see them often enough, I see their smiling faces cross my mind regularly. I hear their voices weekly via texts, email threads and phone calls. We are here for each other and we always will be. Even amidst tears and differences, we add smiles to our lives because of the love we share with one another.

Friends. One day, all of us will get separated from each other. We will miss our conversations. Days, months, and years will pass until we rarely see each other. One day, our children will see our photo and ask, "Who are these people?" And we will smile with invisible tears and say, "It was with them that I had the best days of my life."

Friends are like that, aren't they? Donny and I are so grateful for our friendships, locally and beyond. As we get older, we tend to become stuck in our ways; we're less apt to try new things. We're also more stubborn with our opinions. Indulging in some friend time can avert these changes, as we age. That's because friends help us learn new things about ourselves. They also open us up to new experiences, offering fresh perspectives on problems. Friends help us feel more connected, build our confidence, and help us to smile more in this earthly life we are living. Thank You, to all of our friends who love us just the way we are, warts and all!

In life, it's not where you go, it's who goes with you!

The FFs.

Going forward, how might you and I develop the habit of a ready smile like my Mama? Like my sis, Laura Lea, we may even have to practice in a mirror after brushing our teeth or washing our face. Let's start today.

A Related Blog Post

January 8, 2020

The Day I Rang the Salvation Army Bell With A Ready Smile

Each One Reach One

It may be a distant memory now, but there were some very rainy days in Georgia during the month of December 2019. It is easy to recall driving home slowly from a holiday party and climbing into our warm, comfy bed as soon as possible.

Then my thoughts would begin. "Where are the homeless sleeping tonight on this soggy cold evening? Were there enough beds at the shelter? Are there children out there with their Mommies and Daddies? Will they be okay?"

Then I would utter a brief prayer from my bed. "Please, Lord, keep them safe and help them to find dry shelter and warmth." I knew in my heart, felt compelled in my soul, that He would use me to help those in need somehow, someway during these cold, wet December days.

As the December days clicked by, we held a wonderful caroling gathering at dk Gallery on the last Sunday before Christmas. Our guests brought new socks, underclothes, gloves, hats and scarves. We collected an abundance of these items, wrapped a bow around them individually and delivered them to The Zone. A nearby center, The Zone has programs that fuel recovery and fight addiction. Those who are in the throes of an addiction are often not welcome in their family home during the holidays. Knowing The Zone would be open for 36 hours during Christmas Eve and Christmas Day, feeding all who came by, our small love gifts would be distributed to those who stopped in.

Soon it was Christmas Eve, 2019. Knowing that my last-minute chores were squared away, I stopped by the local Salvation Army office and asked if I could ring a bell. The receptionist told me that no one was ringing at a nearby Wal-Mart on Roswell Road, and would I be willing to work there. My assigned shift was 10:00-1:00, and a Salvation Army representative would meet me there.

Christmas Eve, 2019, Walmart in Marietta, GA.

I arrived a few minutes early. After waiting a good while, the representative never arrived. I tried calling a few numbers, but most offered only a machine since it was Christmas Eve. Sadly, I entered the Wal-Mart to pick up one last thing, potatoes for our Christmas feast.

As soon as I came out, I saw her! A woman was ringing the bell cheerily and walking to and fro on the storefront sidewalk. After introducing myself and acknowledging that there had been some misunderstanding, my new friend offered me the bell and her chair and slipped inside to hang out at the Subway sandwich shop. I was going to get to ring that bell after all!

The next couple of hours, I called out Merry Christmas to all who could hear, offered up a ready smile, and a chocolate Santa to the children. I noticed the variety of nationalities represented, considering my American citizenship

Sadly, I saw a homeless young man searching for food or a tobacco butt in a nearby trash can and ash bin. I offered him a chocolate Santa and he heartily accepted it. (and I sent up an arrow prayer of gratitude that I had never been in this man's shoes) I took in the number of taxi rides folks needed to get the shoppers to and from the store. (and I thought about our pick-up truck in the parking lot full of gas and ready to take me home). I thanked those who slipped small change, a single or a five into the traditional red bucket. As I thanked one woman with her two young children, her reply warmed my heart, "Salvation Army made a real difference in my life in the past, and I want to give back." (and I considered the fact that I had never had to reach out for help like this)

Just as He promised that cold, rainy night when I uttered a short prayer from my bed, I was given the privilege to help some souls in need. My heart was warmed that Christmas Eve and not just by the surprising warmer, sixty-degree Georgia temp and blue sky. It was also warmed by that feeling you get when you've made a difference in someone's life, no matter how small.

I was reminded of that old song first penned in 1955, "Let There Be Peace On Earth and Let It Begin In Me."

Each One Reach One. A smile is a free gift we can offer to others whenever we want to send out cheer and encouragement.

Let's Start Today.

As we have traveled on through Mama's lessons, I see her bright smile in my mind's eye. One integral part of being a grandparent is by offering the littles a smile every chance possible. We will see evidence of this in an upcoming chapter filled with thoughts from the grands. Mama beamed when her many grandchildren were in her midst.

I am so grateful for both of these young men. Walker, holding daughter, Elizabeth and Scott holding son, Tripp. These two guys smile, play with, help with, interact with their children and their wives. They are present passionate providers. These two are the best family men I know!

Mama never allowed the "b-word, bored" with the six of us growing up. And she discouraged the use of this word with the grands, as well. Whether at home or abroad, in Mama's mind, there was always something interesting to notice and to learn about. Mama didn't want to miss a thing. Therefore "living each and every moment" was a preeminent priority for her.

All smiles with my two favorite girls in the world for some birthday fun on Fernandina Beach. August 1, 2017, Leah to my right and Jessica to my left.

TTU ADPi Sisters, 1983 at Leslie's in Knoxville, Tennessee

This group! We've brought each other smiles through the years. We met just out of high school, at Tennessee Tech University in the late 1970s. These Alpha Delta Pi sisters are a treasure to my heart. Getting together every year since meeting has been a tradition for over four decades now. We sustain each other in a slew of ways including prayer, tears, laughter, and adventures through the years. Our precious circle of friends is a steadfast share of our lives.

JoAnn, Susan, Leslie, Kay, Debby, Delores, Becky, Kelly, and Joan.

Together, we've witnessed firsthand this Dolly Parton quote come to light:

> "Storms make trees take deeper roots"
>
> Dolly Parton, (January 19, 1946-) American singer, songwriter, multi-instrumentalist, actress, author, businesswoman, humanitarian.

Here we are at the Dollywood DreamMore Resort on January 31, 2020 in the Great Smokies of Tennessee, before our world was sideswiped with Covid-19.

"Enjoy the little things in life because one day you'll
look back and realize they were the big things."

Kurt Vonnegut

"Life is what happens when you are busy making other plans."

John Lennon

Lesson 11

Live Each Moment

> "I walk about in freedom, for I have sought out your precepts."
>
> —Psalm 119:45

Another way to describe living each moment is to "seize the day." What do those three words mean to you? For me, Mama often modeled to live in the moment that we were actually living in. Did you know? When we pay too much attention to yesterdays and tomorrows, we truly do miss out on our todays.

There is a passage in the Bible that has helped me to live out this lesson the best that I can, and I bet it will help you too. Found in Matthew 6:25–34, this text is all about Jesus, teaching on worrying. While we will consider more about worry in lesson 12, this passage reminds me to live in each moment.

I love all things nature, don't you?

> "Life is too short to wake up in the morning with regrets. So, love the people who treat you right, forgive the ones who don't and believe that everything happens for a reason. If you get the chance, take it. If it changes your life, let it. Nobody said it would be easy, they just promised it would be worth it."
>
> Dr. Seuss

One Saturday morning in October 2020, I was awakened on Lake Blue Ridge to excitement just outside my bedroom window. After two bald eagles were fighting over a live fish, the prizewinner landed on a nearby stoop to kill and eat his prey for breakfast. Our son-in-law, Scott was the discoverer of this magnificent chronicle of events in nature. A story that would have unfolded whether we witnessed it or not. Grabbing my robe and a steaming cup of black coffee, I joined Scott to contemplate this creature. For nearly thirty minutes, the massive white head bobbed up and down devouring the catch. Sharing a pair of binoculars back and forth, we waited in anticipation for the majestic bird to take flight. And when it did, in our estimation, the wingspan measured four to five feet across. Soaring across the surface of the lake, all I could think of was one word: freedom.

Freedom to soar, to live, to be, to speak, to believe, to live in each moment.

The picture below, from 2003, illustrates when my heart began to break apart, then begin to repair. Vera. I was meant to meet Vera on my very first of many trips to Rio de Janeiro.

It is clear in the photo that my heart was broken over the poverty I witnessed. However, here's what I learned. Vera was living in this poverty, in the favelas of Rio. And yet, she carried great joy within herself because of one thing. Actually, because of one person. The person of Jesus Christ. That is freedom. I am learning that freedom is a gift that should never be taken for granted. It is also a concept that means a lot of different things depending on your perspective.

The Bible contains many wise words on the subject of freedom. It is a great resource for understanding the meaning of freedom. Learning how to find it. Cultivating it in your life and in my life. Vera, unforgettable, that's what you are.

Sharing with Vera, a sister-in-Christ.

"...This day is sacred to our Lord. Do not grieve, for the joy of the Lord is your strength." Nehemiah 8:10

My friend, Vera's words in Portuguese interpreted to me in English: "It is better to have nothing and know God than to have wealth and not know God."

October 2003

The official currency in Brazil is the Real, which is pretty straightforward, but many people wonder exactly how to pronounce the "Brazilian real" because when you hear a Brazilian say it, it sounds nothing like that! The answer is that "real" is pronounced "hey-al" and the plural, "reais," is pronounced "hey-ice." I carry this bill in my wallet to remind me to pray for the beautiful Brazilian people. I have grown to love them so much.

I thought of my favorite Rae Dunn oversized coffee mug boasting this one word: FREEDOM.

I thought of The Eagles' hit, "Already Gone" and these lyrics: "So often times it happens that we live our lives in chains and we never even know we have the key."

The aforementioned Matthew passage causes me to take pause, to consider the importance of living in the moment. Like this eagle story, a beautiful example of nature working itself out, Matthew 6 refers to birds, flowers and humans thriving in a not always welcoming world. The birds do not sow or reap or stow away in barns, and even so, their heavenly Father feeds them. The lilies of the fields do not labor or spin, yet their beauty is indescribable. And humans, you and me, we run around after all things. We wonder what we will drink, eat and wear. And verse 33 of this chapter 6 tells us to seek God first and all of these things will be given to us, as well. Living in the moment, not borrowing trouble from tomorrow, or allowing ourselves to live in regrets of yesterday is vital.

From Mama's Journal

October 29, 1981

I cooked nearly all day, soup, roast, brownies, and cake. John W. and Jeanie came about 5:00 p.m. Evan Wade is so cute! He's grown so much since August. He really verbalizes a lot and I think he will talk soon. Laura called and asked if she could invite Rhys over and Joan is bringing Donny. It seems like old times. After dinner,

Johnny went back to hospital and Jeanie got Evan to bed. Laura and Joan and friends were trying to plan Halloween costumes. They have been in the attic. Billy came up with the idea of "Bonnie & Clyde" for Joan and Donny. We found everything they needed except a gun but did find a blonde wig for Joan (Kathy's). Laura and Rhys went as a scarecrow and Little Red Riding Hood. Soon, the girls left, and we went to bed."

From Joan's Journal

Wednesday, January 2, 2013

I awakened raring to go this morning, even though I had a hard time going to sleep last night. So much on my mind...mostly good stuff. One thing I want to do more of in this new year is to watch the sun rise, with hot coffee in hand. The sunrise is due today at 7:43 a.m. so I'll sit here at my desk until then. As I sit, I hear a couple of birds singing loudly, announcing the coming of a new day. The sky is beginning to LIGHT UP.

As I wait, the song we sing in church crosses my mind: "Let Faith Arise." When I am still like this, I feel my faith in God rising up. The sky is brighter, and my soul is lighter. Five minutes 'til sunrise in Marietta, Georgia.

The time has passed with no bright orange ball because of all the rain and the overcast sky. Still, a new day has dawned and as Jeremiah wrote so long ago in Lamentations 3:22–23, "His mercies are new every morning." Thank YOU, Jesus. Now time to get back to undecorating our house! Quite the chore!

I would never suggest that we live out our days by the seat of our pants, haphazard activities one after another. Although, I do love spontaneity. Planning is good and brings a peace about what may be just around the corner. Other than meal planning and a few scheduled events here and there, Mama was not too much of a planner. Mama jotted grocery lists, Bible verses, quotes, and to-do lists out onto scratch paper. I do this, too.

I don't want to miss a thing. I bet you don't either!

The day was October 24, 2018, and I found myself sitting on the grass, up on a gentle hill, beside the graves of both my Mama and my Daddy. A peaceful place, located on the Tennessee Georgia state line about one hundred miles from our home, I began to write in my journal:

> I do not weep for I know they are not there. As I sit here a million thoughts go through my mind...mostly sentiments of pure gratefulness. Mama, I'm still working on my book project about lessons you taught me. I love you both with all of my heart and thank my God every day for the family you formed for all of us. I pray you can see us! Even me right here on the grass. Then I will know that you know about all of our new family members. Mama! I'm a grandmother!

I believe that the following messages join this lesson to live each moment.

Life is fragile. Handle with care and prayer.

Life is short.

Life is beautiful in good times and in difficult times.

Life is a gift.

Life is an adventure.

Life is in the moments of each day.

My sister, Laura Lea has helped to encourage me to live in each moment. An example of this is a bit of musing penned by Laura. The date was October 12, 2020, early morn. While Laura was in

Georgia with her husband, Rhys, I was on Hilton Head Island in South Carolina with my family. As is often the case, our hearts were knitted together in spirit.

I was posting a live sunrise Monday Mood video on my Pages From Joan. Here is what Laura wrote: *"As we watched that Monday Mood, each one of us, in many different places were brought together in awe of our Creator. Spirits soared in silence, as the sun seared the surface over the sea."*

Laura Lea Lamkie

How can you and I make our moments, day by day count? It's been said that this life is not a dress rehearsal, and we only get one chance. Let's live each moment. Let's start today.

A Related Blog Post

February 20, 2017

Let's Live Each Moment!
7 Lifestyle Choices Equals
A Big Difference
Our Health Plan

Here, I will share with you 7 lifestyle choices that = a big difference in your overall health and well-being.

This past Wednesday afternoon, I met my long-time friend, Kathy Owen at the Kennesaw Mountain National Battlefield Park, and we tackled the Mountain Road, approximately 1.4 miles straight up. Then on Friday, I met up with my girlfriend, Rita Maynard, to challenge ourselves at an Orange Theory Fitness West Cobb class with Coach Lou at 7:30 a.m.

Kathy and Joan, Kennesaw Mountain

We love to catch up as we hike up Kennesaw Mountain when my friend, Kathy comes into town from her home in Pensacola, Florida.

Over President's Day weekend, seven of my college ADPi friends came to Marietta and we enjoyed a three-night sleepover! We walked every day, including another trip to the strenuous Mountain Road on Saturday afternoon. Time spent with friends is good for the heart.

I am more personally motivated than ever before after listening to our friend, Dr. William A. Cooper do a Q/A on Facebook Live regarding cardiac health, lifestyle choices, and how you and I can directly impact our life with a few changes. Not only is William a Cardiothoracic Surgeon (an open-heart surgery doc), but he is also a friend, an author, and a visionary leader who is very motivated to help lay people like you and me lead healthier lives.

You see, sadly, William has learned first-hand about loss and disease in his own family: his dear Mom died from cancer at age 46, a sis, age 27, diabetes, another sis, 41, heart disease, a brother, age 45, heart, another brother, age 53, AIDS, and another sis, age 58, cancer! Now, Dr. Cooper, a veteran who was deployed to Iraq and Afghanistan, has dedicated himself to combating heart disease through education and prevention. He is growing more and more passionate about helping as many humans as possible to get serious about their personal health plan. Dr. Cooper's book is called Heart Attack: Truth*Tragedy*Triumph.

William started this particular Q/A I heard a few Saturdays ago with this question:

"What is your personal health plan?"

In answer to this question, many might think Dr. Cooper is referring to your insurance health plan, but he isn't! He is talking about choices you and I make moment by moment, day by day which greatly impact our wellness.

Following are the 7 lifestyle choices that were discussed:

(1) Control stress, stress is the reason we overeat, overdrink, don't workout, smoke and have other addictive behaviors. Let's take time to be still enough to ask ourselves the question:

"Am I stressed? If I am, what do I intend to do about it?"

(2) Control/Reduce Sugar. Read labels and when you read 'high fructose', avoid it. Manage your diet and your intake.

(3) Get weight down to a healthy level with nutritional management. Leave

saltshakers behind and use more natural herbs, pepper, and turmeric for seasoning.

(4) Move to a largely plant-based diet.

(5) After age 40, know your blood pressure numbers and your cholesterol numbers.

(6) See your doctor. When we know we are unhealthy, it is easy to procrastinate about this, but your M.D. cannot help you if you do not go in to see him/her.

(7) Exercise 30 minutes minimum each day to achieve target heart rate. Consider getting a buddy to walk with and catch up while getting fit! Find an activity you enjoy and just do it. A healthy outside starts from the inside.

Here with our college buddy, Kay, Paul Read is always helping someone ready their bike for Taylor's Annual Ride on the Virginia Creeper Trail ride. Abingdon, VA.

A few more things I wrote down during Dr. Coop's Q/A:

* Change your eating habits.
* We eat too many of the wrong things at the wrong time.
* Eat protein/high fat before 6 p.m.
* Match caloric intake for when you are the most active.

In addition to Dr. Cooper's book, I have learned so much from a book, Younger Next Year For Women (there's a bright yellow one for men, too!) It is humorous and helpful at the same time!

"Okay, you're a terrific woman, maybe in your late forties, maybe your early sixties, and your life has gone pretty well. You have good energy, decent gifts, and right now you seem to be heading into a particularly nice stretch. The kids are getting big or are gone. Old Fred, if he's around, is taking care of himself, and the relationship is taking some nice turns, getting a little calmer. For some reason—menopause or whatever—you feel as if it's time, at long last, to look after yourself and your own, serious business. Time to take your own affairs, your own life, your own needs in hand and do something. Maybe something pretty big."

Chris Crowley, co-author of Younger Next Year

What will you and I do in the weeks and months ahead to improve our health plan? Whatever we do to improve our health will surely help us to better live each moment!

During the last weeks of Mama's earthly life, a continuous outpouring of family members came by their apartment in Cartersville, Georgia. On a particular October afternoon, several of The Seder Family members filed in and out of the bedroom offering hugs and utterances of pure love. With them, was one of Mama's son-in-law's, Jim, there to say his good-byes. After spending a few quiet minutes at the bedside, Jim turned to leave. Mama called to him, saying, "Jim." As he turned around to meet her gaze, she continued, "We had fun didn't we!?!"

Living each moment has become more and more important to me. As I have entered my sixth decade of life, I truly want to follow my Mama's final lesson as closely as possible.

Though it is easier said than done, feeling anxious about some future event or circumstance does me no good. Worrying does not increase the chances of a good outcome. Mama taught us all to never borrow trouble from tomorrow. Read on to see how she actually did this very thing as she lived out her days.

"Worrying is like a rocking chair, it gives you something to do, but it gets you nowhere." Erma Bombeck

"Worry often gives a small thing a big shadow." Swedish Proverb

"Worrying never robs tomorrow of its sorrow, it only saps today of its joy." Leo F. Buscaglia

Lesson 12

Don't Borrow Trouble From Tomorrow

This is a big and important lesson. One I likely attempt to apply on a daily basis. Why do we worry so much in life? Is worrying simply part of being human? Mama didn't think so. Mama believed that worrying got her nowhere and therefore she made it a regular habit to never allow herself to borrow trouble from tomorrow. In fact, she often quipped a version of the Erma Bombeck quote above since one of her favorite pastimes was rocking babies!

The 2020 United States presidential election has been decided as of the past few days. Former Vice President, Joe Biden will be sworn in as our forty-sixth president on January 20, 2021. Regardless of who you and I supported during this tumultuous election, it is clear to all watching both here and abroad that there is currently a colossal divide between the American people. A massive mountain of difference and belief in what the future of the United States should look like.

Have you and I ever stopped and wondered what our parents and friends who have gone on ahead of us might have to say about all of the current turmoil? I have asked myself this often, actually, "What would Mama and Daddy have to say about _____?"

And I believe in my heart that Mama would say, "Honey, we can't borrow trouble from tomorrow." Because no matter who we support in an election, between the newly elected senate and a change of office in our presidency, there will be many changes. Hopefully, more positive than not. And then Mama would remind us to pray for our president and the administration. Mama believed wholeheartedly in the power of her humble prayers.

Uncertainty may cause us to borrow trouble from tomorrow, right? During this, still ongoing, global pandemic, there has been an overabundance of uncertainty. Much of which has not been fun or enjoyable. And yet, as we look ("search") for favorable facets of this year, we will find some. We will. Families have bonded. Heroes have been spotlighted. Faith and hope have swelled. The preciousness, the fragility of life has been underscored. Scientists have worked harder than before to find a viable solution. And many more irrefutable images come to mind that linger inside our souls. Unforgettable soul snapshots.

We simply must refuse to waste energy worrying. When we intentionally dismiss distress, we will have more strength to spare. It's been said that change is the only constant in life. If this is true, then we have yet another motive to not borrow trouble from the future.

Recognizing that change is constantly occurring makes me think of the "Whack-a-Mole" game in the Suburban Plaza Bowling Alley Arcades when I was growing up. Five holes in the play area top are filled with small plastic moles, which pop up at random. Points are scored by whacking each mole with a soft, black mallet as it appears. The object was to knock the moles down as soon as you saw them. The faster the reaction the higher the score.

This journey called life is kind of like that. Once we get one problem under control and working, another life issue rears its head…just like the arcade game.

I don't know about you, but I am learning that evolving, ever-changing life circumstances have taught me to look up, with humility to my God, in faith.

My long-time, dear friend, Marie Corrigan, has dealt with a chronic, life-threatening illness for a decade now. Every time, we chat she says, *"Joan, I'm still chasing after Jesus!"*

Marie Corrigan

Marie Corrigan, founder of Sophia Academy, Atlanta, Georgia. Marie and I first met in 1983, had our babies together, and have helped each other during good times and bad.

Did you know? There are more than eighty-five verses in the Bible that promise the reader that when we seek God, we will find Him every time. Every time. And I have found this to be true in my faith journey. First Peter 5:7 reminds us to cast ALL of our burdens onto God because He cares for us. Seeking God is salve for my soul. It is fuel for my faith. It is pure joy and encouragement for my journey. It is the name of my Daddy's favorite hymn: "Blessed Assurance."

> "Though it is easier said than done, feeling anxious about some future event or circumstance does me no good. Worrying does not increase the chances of a good outcome."
>
> Anonymous

Especially in these turbulent times across our globe, I am wondering if you experience this comfort in your soul. This same equanimity as my girlfriend, Marie. Even amidst the health battle of her life. If not, why not? Have you asked yourself this question?

I recognize that multitudes of Christians have damaged the name of Christ. I do see this. And sadly, I am certain that I have, as well. Author, Madeline L'Engle had this to say about Christianity, "We do not draw people to Christ by loudly discrediting what they believe, by telling them how wrong they are and how right we are, but by showing them a light that is so lovely that they want with all their hearts to know the source of it."

First, as a young girl of age nine, and overtime in my heart of hearts, I have grown closer to the heart of my God, Creator. I have come to claim His Name as my Shepherd, my Comforter, my Blessed Redeemer, my Counselor, my Advocate. The one who goes ahead of me in every circumstance of my life, known and unknown.

This reminds me of the story of a very young Corrie ten Boom when it was time for her to take a trip on a train. One of my favorite, most inspiring humans, Corrie ten Boom was born in 1892. A Dutch Christian, along with her father and sister, Corrie courageously hid Jews in their home during the Second World War. Her family was betrayed and handed over to the Germans, and they were sent to the notorious Ravensbruck Concentration Camp. While there, both Corrie's father and sister, Betsy, passed away. Even with these tremendous losses, Corrie did not lose her grip on God. When she was finally released, because of a clerical error, Corrie would often reflect on the truth that it was her God that had given her the strength to endure these horrific circumstances. It was God who supplied his sufficient grace precisely when she needed it.

Corrie actually learned this very early in her life in the midst of death. When she was a young girl, Corrie witnessed the death of a baby, confronted by the fragile nature of life. Frightened by this experience, she burst into tears, she sobbed to her daddy. "I need you. You can't die! You can't!" Desiring to soothe his anxious child, he sat down beside her and gently said, "Corrie, when you and I travel to

Amsterdam, when do I give you the ticket?" Wiping her nose, she answered, "Just before we get on the train."

"Exactly," her daddy responded with love, "and our wise Father in heaven knows when we are going to need things too. Let's not run ahead of God, Corrie. When the time comes for us to die, you will look into your heart and find the strength you need, just in time."

Corrie ten Boom learned something that day that would hold true throughout her life. She went onto live ninety-one years, passing onto eternity on her birthday, April 15. God doesn't give us grace for the future. Just like manna, in the Old Testament, grace cannot be stored. It must be used for the moment we are in and nothing more. Yes, grace is like the manna God supplied the Israelites in the wilderness. Just like the food in our fridge and our pantries, grace has an expiration date on it. Its shelf life is one day (Exod. 16:21). Grace is for right now (2 Cor. 12:9).

Sure, like Corrie, it is simpler to let our minds run ahead of us, causing a flood of fears. It is human nature for us to wonder about tomorrow, however God has promised us strength for each new day (Deut. 33:25). There is no grace for tomorrow until tomorrow. I am learning that one of the secrets to successful living is living in the moment of God's abundant and extraordinary grace. Thank you, Lord.

He is my reason that I live out my days following this lesson my Mama taught me, to not borrow trouble from tomorrow.

We are a part of a church family in Marietta, Georgia that exists to exhibit love and light to others.

Our Pastor Ike Reighard, the staff, along with our Piedmont Church small group have given us strength for our earthly meandering. Studying God's Word with these longtime friends has sustained us in more ways than we can express. Afterall, we are just sojourners here.

And we are all just walking each other home.

Thank YOU, Lord!

Piedmont Church Ladies' Retreats, Lake Blue Ridge. 2016 and 2019. As fellow believers, these gatherings are salve for our souls.

We do not have to borrow trouble from tomorrow. Your future needs you. Your past does not. Let's live this day, while there is still daylight.

Let us all stop borrowing trouble from tomorrow. Let's start today.

A Related Blog Post

> *January 11, 2016*
>
> Don't Borrow Trouble
> He Is My Anchor
>
> Many of you know that I started this blog in memory of my Mama who passed away in 2006. Esophageal Cancer took her from us just four short months after her diagnosis. Mom was

239

78. Even when she found out about her illness, her first response was: "Well, we're supposed to bloom where we're planted, aren't we?" Mama made it a habit to not borrow trouble often using the word "concerned" in lieu of "worried".

Adopted at age three, Mama went on to marry, Johnny, the love of her life at age 21 and live an extraordinary life, impacting others for good wherever she turned. Multitudes have been blessed with her memory, her heritage, including six grown, married children, twenty-six grands and twelve great-grands. A legacy like Mama's lives on forever!

I can honestly say that I think of my Mama every single day, and I probably always will. One reason my thoughts go to her is because of the many life mantras she lived out during our days shared together.

One of these which I consider often is "Don't borrow trouble from tomorrow by worrying." This brief nugget of wisdom can be applied to so many moments in our lives.

Is someone making a long trip and you are hoping for traveling mercies? Do you have a family member who is sick, and you don't know how to best help them? Is someone you love expecting a child and you are praying for a safe delivery? Has your child left for college and now, you have no clue what his/her days and nights look like? Is someone you adore suffering with the disease of addiction? Are you having communication issues with a close relationship and you are unsure how it will turn out? Do you have uncertain circumstances coming up in your journey? Are you and your sweetheart planning to start a family and the timing is not what you had thought it would be?

> "Pray without ceasing." 1 Thessalonians 5:17

Have you had a recent surgery, are you going through physical therapy and you are not sure if you are healing well? Are you wondering how that "special wedding day" will turn out, that day you all have planned extensively for? Are you having health issues and you are not sure which direction to turn? Is a beloved one away serving in our military? Has someone dear to your heart passed recently, leaving you wondering how you will keep living?

What might you add to this list that you find yourself worrying about?

Borrowing trouble from tomorrow is a bad kind of debt because it is "borrowing" with absolutely no pay-off whatsoever. Worry is often the nonacceptance of circumstances that you cannot do anything about. Even the Bible reminds us to not borrow trouble from tomorrow. See Matthew 6:25-34.

The Serenity Prayer helps me so much as I continue to desire days where I do not borrow any trouble from tomorrow:

The Full Serenity Prayer
God grant me the serenity
To accept the things I cannot change;
Courage to change the things I can;
And wisdom to know the difference.
Living one day at a time;
Enjoying one moment at a time;
Accepting hardships as the pathway to peace;

Taking, as He did, this sinful world
As it is, not as I would have it;
Trusting that He will make things right
If I surrender to His Will;
So that I may be reasonably happy in this life
And supremely happy with Him
Forever and ever in the next.
Amen.
How will you and I avoid borrowing trouble
from tomorrow
in the days, weeks and months ahead?
Let's Start Today.

I wonder when Mama decided it was useless to worry about the future.

Mama had a chance to practice this lesson to the fullest extent back in 1972 at the age of forty-four. Her love, Johnny, and her oldest daughter, Mary Ann, a nurse returned to Africa to work for a couple of weeks. According to her journal entry, there were plenty of uncertainties and more than enough chances to borrow trouble from tomorrow.

From Mama's Journal

September 10, 1972

4:30 a.m. Johnny and Mary Ann just called from Africa. It was a very short three minutes, unbelievable. It is wonderful to hear from them, but it makes me want to see them more. I called Jim about 8:30 a.m. He called Mary Ann. It was about 1:30 there and they are to leave Africa tonight. I am not sure of the time. This is Mary Ann's 21st birthday. They will arrive in N.Y. between 1 and 2 a.m. I am so excited about tomorrow. The children want to go to airport, and I will let them if possible.

I set the clock between 1 and 2, but no call from Johnny. I reset the alarm for six to awaken the children. No news from N.Y.

I am really not worried, but I would like to hear something. Got the kids off to school. They were disappointed not to go to airport. No news at 8:30 a.m. Johnny and Mary Ann called from N.Y. They were delayed in West Africa for one hour. They will arrive in Atlanta at 1:30. I called Jim to notify him. Needless to say, he was relieved. Their plane was on time, and it was wonderful to see them again. They are very tired, but also very excited about their adventure. It is wonderful to be with Johnny again. Mary Ann went to pick up Billy for football practice."

From Joan's Journal

Thursday, August 6, 2009

I am at the Cobb County Kemp Library preparing the next three Thursday night Bible Studies on the Gospel of John. I am praying for discernment, wisdom, and God's Love as I lead a few Marietta girlfriends through John. My eyes tear up as I remember Jil, yesterday, the 4th anniversary of her passing on 8/5/2005. I remember us going through John together, just the two of us, chapter-by-chapter, in our living room of our Brookstone home. God led me then and I know He will lead me now.

'Yet the timeless in you is aware of life's timelessness, and knows that yesterday is but today's memory and tomorrow is today's dream.'

Copied from The Prophet by, Kahil Gibran.

I used the above quote in my blog post today! The title of the post was LET IT GO!

I walked five miles in the woods today with Gracie and Mocha. YES, for Growth!

Our journey through Mama's Lessons is drawing to an end.

I am so glad you joined me on this trip down our family's memory lane. Before we bring our time to a close, you will read a few more sections, some tender-hearted thoughts. Musings about Polly from men who loved her, reminiscences and remembrances from the grandchildren, and some pretty cool and useful lessons from other mothers.

Just some of our fun, crazy, extraordinary extended family, December 2016. Photo Credit, photographer, Dixie Buice.

Reflections from a Few Men
Who Knew and Loved Polly

Polly Shivers Walker, 1997
Mama Loved the Lord
John Wade Walker, III

John Wade

J o Nelle (Polly) Gordon Shivers Walker, my Mama, loved the Lord.
She loved her family, her husband, her children, and her grandchildren. She also loved the wives and the husbands of her children.
"Magnolia Steel," soft as the Mississippi state flower, but with a
strong will and determination.

Mama never knew a stranger.

Mama enjoyed life to its fullest, laughed often, sharing her happiness with others. She read her Bible daily and shared the joy and pain of those who came to her. Mama was a Good Listener, and others were comfortable talking with her. She was a voracious reader, loving all books. Mama enjoyed jigsaw puzzles and playing Canasta. Mama and Dad both had a strong empathy for others. As a Nurse and a Doctor, they served in Africa as Medical Missionaries for four years. She was a strong marriage partner for our Father as she supported him well. They both believed in prolife, and belonged to organizations that supported this view. They were both members of "Parents of Marines," supporting those parents who had lost their sons in Vietnam. Mama frequently brought strength and comfort to others. Having an "attitude of gratitude," Mama was always thankful for her blessings. In her later years, as her health was failing, Mama exemplified a "quiet strength." She held great confidence that she would join other family members in the "Arms of our Lord." Mama was a fighter, always ready to face any battle because of her faith and spiritual strength.

I liken my Mama to the Spartan mother preparing her son for battle: "Come home carrying your shield or be carried back on it."

A quick, true story: My college roommate had come to visit our home for the weekend. He had a huge, canvas duffle bag containing all of his dirty laundry. He handed the heavy bag to our Mother to wash and dry his clothes. Without skipping a beat, Mama kicked the bag down the basement steps, smiled, telling our "guest," "The washer and dryer are downstairs. Do your own damn laundry."

End of story.

In closing, Billy always said Mama is in heaven rocking babies, and this is an image we all hold close to our hearts.

Stories from the Youngest
William Shivers Walker

Billy

How do I begin telling stories about the funniest lady I have ever met? I guess I just begin. At Webster Drive, we had two cats, Mutt and Jeff, in addition to a pair of Boston Terriers, Beau and Belle. Well, one day, Mama came into the kitchen and found Mutt chowing down on the Sunday pot roast that had been left in the kitchen sink to cool. Thinking the back door was wide open, Mama grabbed Mutt by the tail and flung him toward the door. The cat slid down the door just like in the cartoon. I don't think Mutt ever tried that again.

Mom knew I loved wild critters of all kinds. Therefore, she allowed me to keep in the house any that I found. Whether it was a snake, bullfrog, or something else, as long as I kept it in a cage, I was free to adopt it as my own. One day, my friends and I found a baby alligator in the pond at Candler Park. After bringing it home, it wouldn't eat. Mom wanted to help me, so she chopped up some ham for it. That was a good idea. The alligator liked it so much, it bit my finger. Ouch!

Continuing with reptile reports, Mom and I were traveling alone to Callaway Gardens one night. We were going to stay a few days at our home at Pine Mountain Club Chalets. Showing up right in the middle of the road was a six-foot king snake! We stopped the car, and Mom let me get out and capture it. Not knowing what to do with it, she suggested I empty Dad's gym bag that was in the trunk. Out flew Dad's tennis shoes, a sweat towel, and a change of clothes. In went the snake with a quick zip to make sure it stayed inside for the rest of our trip! The next week, I donated the big snake to Fernbank Science Center.

On that same trip, I enjoyed one of my favorite past times, gigging huge catfish that wandered too close to the bank. Nighttime was best. As soon as I crept to the bank, they'd go swiftly to the center of the pond. I would hold really still until they returned to the bank. After I successfully gigged a sixteen-inch catch, I carried it to the house, plopped it on the porch. We would soon clean and scale it. Mom would cut the catfish into chunks, frying it up with homemade french-fries. Now that was a delicious meal!

Surprisingly, Mama did not get her driver's license until she was around the age of thirty-seven. I was in kindergarten. I recall when our car was packed with a crew of Kindergarteners like me. Mama had to slam on the brakes to avoid an accident. Thanks, Mom.

All six of us have a favorite memory I have to share. Daddy had a super big video camera back in the sixties, and he loved to shoot family videos. Our parents would set up a massive box (the size that a new washing machine came in). When the camera was off, Daddy climbs in. Camera on, Daddy climbs out while Mom tapes it. Camera off. Mama climbs in. Camera on. Mama climbs out, nearly tipping the box over and falling. Mom is laughing heartily the entire time. Camera off. John Wade climbs in. Camera on. John raises his arms and jumps out of the box. Then Mary Ann, Kathy, and Laura. Then Joan would hold up her arms for help because she was too small to climb out. Then of course, I was also too little to climb out, and had to be lifted out. In the end… Mary Ann and Kathy held up the big box for all to see that there was a bottom and there was nothing left in it. Just like magic! You'd honestly have to see it to believe it.

It was the first time Lisa and I made our trek down to rural Mississippi to visit my parents. Dad and I immediately went out to wet a line. Mama said, "Come on, Lisa, let's run to the Country Store!" They always made us feel so at home. While I would walk around the lakes looking for snakes and other critters, Mama and Lisa would catch up. Those were good days.

I will never forget the feeling I had back in 2006 when Mama called me to tell me about her cancer. I was driving my Silverado pickup truck. I told Mama I had to go, I had to call her back later. I pulled over to the side of the road and cried.

A Very Special Lady!
James R. Elrod

Jim

A very special lady, a wife, a mom, and a mother-in-law. You were always welcomed in her home with a smile, a hug, and a kind word.

She and I connected in a special way. We were able to celebrate our birthdays together. December 20.

One special birthday was her seventy-fifth. We took her and GoodDaddy to New York City. We stayed at the Downtown Hilton in New York City for several days. We walked to Times Square (pushed her in a wheelchair). Saw the Rockettes perform the Christmas Special at Radio City Music Hall. We also went to a Broadway Show.

One highlight was eating dinner in China Town. After dinner, we went out to catch a taxi back to the hotel, easier said than done. It had rained and we started to wave down a taxi to no avail. After many attempts, GoodDaddy steps off the sidewalk in between two parked cars to stop a taxi. He suddenly realized he had stepped into an eight-inch deep pothole full of water. I let go of the wheelchair to grab Dad and turned around and saw GoodMama rolling down the hill on the sidewalk in the wheelchair laughing and enjoying the ride.

The evening ended with many laughs and no crashes however, one wet shoe. She always made you feel good and happy, no matter the circumstances.

My First Memory of Polly (Spring 1979)

Donald A. Page Jr.

Donny

One of my favorite memories of Polly occurred when Joan and I first started dating. Joan had invited me to the family home in Decatur for the first time. I was on my way home from college to my hometown of Thomaston, Georgia for the weekend. I had my dog, Bardot with me and as I knocked on the door, Polly opened the door with a broom in her hands. As Bardot ran into the house, she immediately mistook Bardot for a neighbor dog, pushing the broom toward her trying to get her to leave! Needless to say, this could've been a very awkward situation, but Joan quickly explained to her Mom that Bardot was mine. For the first time, I experienced that famous Polly laugh and from then on, we would share many laughs together. Polly always made me feel welcome and loved in the Walker home. There was always a delicious bounty of food at 655 Webster Drive and as a student, this was wonderful! Polly was the best mother-in-law one could ever hope for.

Thoughts from the Grands

Remembrances and Reminiscences

Mama loved her grandchildren and her great-grandchildren, that was for sure. But here's the thing, no matter how many she had, her excitement over the birth of another one never faltered. Here she is in 1999, with the birth of number 16, Billy and Lisa's number one, Jillian, with awe in her eyes. Little sis, Caroline, number 17 followed in 2002 and she loved these two more than ever!

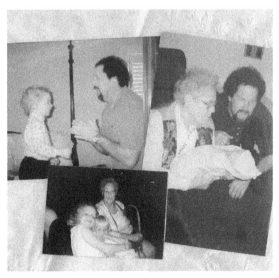

Mama and Daddy added ten grands to their lives during the
decade from 1980 until 1988. Remember how I said I loved being
an aunt before I became a Mommy in 1988? Well, these two
grands were born close together in 1986, and now they are both married!
Emily Seder Cooke and Pamela Lamkie Plott.

Several pairs of grandchildren were born in the same year, like our grandchildren, Tripp and Elizabeth were born two weeks apart in 2018.

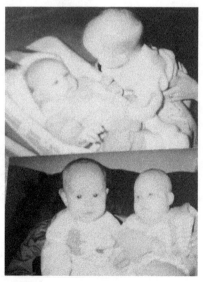

Both entering the world in different states in 1988, Rachael Walker and Leah Page meet for the first time!

Also born in the same year: Amy Elrod Fairchild and Evan Wade Walker, Emily Seder Cooke and Pamela Lamkie Plott, as well as Katie Seder Findlan and Bradford Gordon Lamkie.

The first time Mom and Dad kept Evan and Amy for the weekend, Mama said she had not prayed enough for mothers of twins. I now know what she meant!

Evan Wade Walker

When my Aunt Joan asked me for my remembrances, so many thoughts came into my mind. I immediately thought of the following verse as I reflected on the life of my paternal grandmother:

> "For all people walk each in the name of his
> god, but we will walk in the name of the LORD
> our God forever and ever."

Micah 4:5.

Rachael Lin Walker

As a child, we would visit my grandparents on Silver Run Lake. The memories I have are simple and ordinary. My sister, Savannah and I would eat blueberries off the front bushes. I would watch crawfish burrow into the mud and baby turtles swim around the dock. I remember singing with my brother, Evan while roller skating down the road. The Swan man would bring us frozen fries and pizzas. We would get into the hot tub when it was only half uncovered and dare each other to swim under the other half. GoodMama would make soup (all Walkers eat soup) and play Monopoly with us on the card table. Once she gave my brother a Far Side book. They laughed together. GoodMama laughed a lot. While GoodDaddy was fishing or playing his clarinet with his tape player, GoodMama would take my sister and I to the corner store and buy us ten cent Avon lipstick samples. I remember GoodMama sitting in her chair reading or cross stitching. The big windows behind her had the view of the lake. She was content with herself and happy. When GoodMama laughed she had eyes like my Daddy. She cussed and loved the Lord and I loved her. Her warmth was felt in her home. Together we had ordinary days with kindness, the perfect kind of memories.

Shane Seder

Mom and Dad's first grandchild, Shane Edward Seder, son of Kathy and Jim Seder and big brother to Luke, Katie, Emily, Kevin, and Chad, wrote the following as a Eulogy for Daddy's service held on November 13, 2013:

GoodMama and one of her Great-Grandchildren, Kayla Seder.

"GoodDaddy" and "GoodMomma" are the names I gave my grandparents. When I was little, my parents were trying to teach me to say "GrandDaddy" and "GrandMomma." But when I spoke, "GoodDaddy" and "GoodMomma" came out instead. Our grand-parents loved the name, so it stuck.

It was a long time before I realized that my grandparents had a special name. When I asked my friends about their GoodDaddy and GoodMomma they returned puzzled looks and seemed clueless as to what I was asking. Until that moment, I thought everyone's grandparents were named GoodDaddy and GoodMomma. That is the first time I realized how special my grandparents are.

Our grandparents are so special that words cannot describe them. Our grandparents live a Christ-like life exemplary to me, our family, and the entire world. Our Grandparents have done countless acts in the love of Christ to help our fellow descendants of Adam and Eve all over the Earth. GoodDaddy and GoodMomma look past earthly barriers and only see the image of God in each person. Most people that need to be reached by the Blood of Jesus and saved are not inside of a church. GoodDaddy and GoodMomma didn't just sit in church talking about the great commission they left to GO and live the great commission (Matthew 28:16–20).

If everyone was an example of the Christian life our grandparents demonstrated, the world would be a lot closer to heaven: more people would accept the gift of salvation and the population of heaven would increase beyond our imagination. This is the legacy of our GoodDaddy and GoodMomma—we are that legacy. The great commission given to us by our Lord Jesus Christ in accordance with The Word of Our God. Beware that even when our soul is saved by Jesus, the devil, and his helpers—the enemy—(who have already lost the battle for our salvation) will still seek to keep us from fully realizing the gift Christ has given us thru his sacrifice on the Cross. The enemy seeks to stop us from carrying out the great commission-causing us to give up our legacy. The enemy does this out of vengefulness to keep us from Glorying God. Amen.

I do not refer to GoodDaddy and GoodMomma as "gone." GoodMomma and GoodDaddy live an everlasting life through the gift of salvation. They now worship God together and wait on us in paradise. You can have this same salvation if you confess and call upon the name of Jesus.

"For God so loved the world that he gave
his one and only Son, that whoever believes in
him shall not perish but have eternal life."

John 3:16

"SOME"
of the grand kids
December '90

<u>Katie Seder Findlan</u>

During the summer, we would visit GoodDaddy and GoodMomma in Mississippi. GoodMomma always took us to bingo night, which was so much fun!

On the way there, she would drive really slow on the dirt road and let us ride on the hood of her car! She always wanted everyone to live life to the fullest!

Luke Evan Seder

GoodMomma always lived her life with an abundance of passion and purpose. She could easily liven up a room full of family members with just a smile and her contagious laughter.

Summers were so much fun when our family could visit the grandparents in Silver Run, Mississippi. Grandchildren would be fishing with GoodDaddy on the dock, while GoodMomma would be inside making her decadent Mississippi mud pie.

GoodMomma also loved socializing with neighbors and friends on Bingo night in the Silver Run Lake community. She enjoyed talking with strangers and making them new friends. We have all been blessed to know her and get to spend time with her.

Emily Seder Cooke

Writings from my college days:

Polly whistled Frank Sinatra songs well into the twenty-first century; at grocery stores, at red lights. She had married a doctor and pursued mission work as his nurse in the Belgian Congo. Rocking African babies in between the births of her own, six.

She was an adopted, curly-headed feisty one that lost her vibrant looks as she got older and sicker; until her color faded and she was recognized only by the inherent hunger in her eyes, that wild in her gaze.

On my grandmother's death bed, I played Sinatra on the record player in her empty room. An attempt to submerge the silences and stifle the forthcoming facts. Shortly thereafter, she was carried into rest. Fragile and weak, I shuddered; ashamed of the calamity I had initiated contrasted to the somber that had become a diminishing life. Forever humbled, in her presence, by an abounded legacy.

Amid the caroling of "I've Got a Crush on You" inevitably ascending a woman of the forties back into her ripe years, I sheepishly asked, "Would you like me to turn it off?" down casting my eyes away, knowing like an oracle her rushed fate, but "No!" she commanded, rattling the windows with that innate fire, that rush that no one in all her years of rejoices and adversities had been able to damper out:

Lying back in her bed, she closed her eyes, descending into another life: maybe back into the Fall woods of Mississippi playing running back for three big brothers, amused she could do it all over again, smiled and whispered: "Turn it up."

Emily Seder Cooke: Memories/blurbs taken from "Daughter of a King" essay written in college

The green water scared me. I saw what my grandmother called "sponges" and lied on the dock with the sun reddening my legs. How can those pink blobs be alive? I turned to the white-haired lady sitting in the lawn chair behind me with a great brick home sneaking up behind her, "Goodmomma, are those the sponges you clean dishes with?" I couldn't see her eyes behind her black sunglasses, but her eminent loud laugh worried a timid duck and she lifted her sweet tea into the air, "No, of course not!" I was relieved and confused. I dipped a finger into the cold water and quickly retrieved it out. I smiled to myself for my bravery and returned to pressing the hot wood against my small body, staring down into the murky waters.

♥

"Who wants an ice cream sandwich!" Goodmomma shouted, "Me!" several voices replied. "Don't tell your Momma!" My brothers and sister and I devoured ice cream sandwiches until we all had black mustaches. It was 9 A.M. Afterward, I changed into my flowered bathing suit and eased into the sizzling hot tub. I imagined there were sponges on the bottom and lifted my feet up anxiously. "Goodmomma, can you get in the hot tub with me?" She wore a black bathing suit with big purple flowers and a skirted bottom to assist in covering her large body. She got in and the boiling water rose up to my neck. The sponges were sure to get me then, so I clung to her arm and lied as long as I could floating on my back, staring up to the patio ceiling, wondering all the while if I would crinkle like a raisin from the sponge's poison.

♥

Thursday night's meant BINGO. I'd sit between different old people every week. A good many of the women smelled of Cedar and the men of black licorice and cigars. It's those summer nights in Mississippi, with a child swinging her legs to the tone of an announcer in a white Baptist church, that curtsey my reminiscences when Momma opens the hood of the Cedar chest to retrieve some worn old quilt. I can smell those scents today, and I remember so well it pains my loss of virtue since; having known too much of a telling world. "Goodmomma, can I just yell out BINGO! And win?" Then I'd hear laughs like sandpaper and my grandmother's musical hilarity above all others, and I'd sink down in my chair, and cover my leaking smile with both hands, never sure what was so funny.

♥

It was the 4th of July and Goodmomma had been reading "Southern Living" regularly.

She made an American flag cake with whipped cream and strawberries and blueberries for the red and blue stripes that she tore out a picture of. It inducted a tradition. She didn't even have a bite. I hardly saw her eat many sweets. She was always dieting. The first Slimfast I ever had I got from my grandmother's house. It looked like a milkshake to me, but tasted much worse. She said "If I knew I was gonna live this long, I would have taken better care of my body!" But I loved the softness when I leaned on her, I liked that I could never quite reach my arms all the way around so I had to press closer. She smelled soft, like baby powder and I could inhale the richness and comfort all at once when she hugged me. She was a woman who had read too many magazines, but had also attended too many church services. She was a brazen peanut trapped within a swollen peanut shell. She hung a wooden picture on the wall in her bathroom with a large woman standing on a scale, "Oh Hell!" it said with the shocked fattie gawking downward. It was the image she had of herself which she hated most, but I could not have appreciated the elasticity of aged skin, the softness of white lotions any other way any better. Her presence could not be surpassed, as much her body struggled to compete.

♥

We were on the way to buy worms for the fishing. We always went to this wooden shop nearby. The size of a small bedroom, it had all the worms in the world and smelled like fish. It housed poor, doomed critters but I loved it there—it was like a zoo to a city girl. On the way back, we stopped at a four-way stop on a dusty road and waited for a small, yellow truck to pass. GoodMomma was always giving something when she could, the right away even, because she had the sort of heart where she'd feel guilty if she didn't. But when the pastel, two-door automobile didn't go, Goodmomma did. She told me, "I only have two speeds: fast and stop!" A split second later and I felt a light impact hit the back of the car. I didn't even gasp at the surprise, just opened my mouth and smirked a little. I felt badly for the old man in the green fishing hat. Still stunned by the audacity of an old, Southern woman; he looked afraid. But Goodmomma was all smiles and laughter; it had been an adventure. "Are you okay honey?" my worried mother asked on the other end of the phone line. I looked to my grandmother with wide eyes and grinned.

♥

She was deemed "Best Neighbor" in the local newspaper and I thought I was famous. Her community gushed of how she bought groceries for the ill, cooked and delivered soups selflessly, and could keep anyone's spirit higher than the Mississippi pines. I showed the paper to my disinterested friends, "That's my grandmother" I beamed and pointed to the laughing woman, faded in the grayness of the paper. They ran off and I stood alone under the shadow of a metal slide. I folded up the black and white paper, shoved it into my pocket, and chased after them.

♥

It was a sad day to find out that Goodmomma and Gooddaddy sold their lake house in Mississippi and moved to a small community neighborhood in Cartersville, Georgia. They wanted to be closer to the family, but I missed fishing off the dock, eating homemade peanut butter Chex mix on the kitchen bar stool that spun around, and sticking my small face between the stair rails—watching my parents and grandparents laugh at a world that didn't make sense while they thought I was asleep.

♥

"Which dress do you like better Goodmomma?" "I like the purple. No, actually I like them both, let's get them both. You need a new bathing suit also Emlay." Goodmomma would sit in a chair outside the changing room while my sister and I gathered all the clothes we could to model for her. She bought us whatever we both could agree on which accounted for a different sort of wardrobe that I loved—typically knee-length, high neck dresses with business-like patterns and earth-toned colors. But I could try on almost anything purple, and I knew she'd approve.

♥

"Unforgettable that's what you are. Unforgettable though near or far. Like a song of love that clings to me, how the thought of you does things to me. Never before has someone been more…unforgettable in every way. And forevermore that's how you'll stay" Gooddaddy would sing between quivering blows on his clarinet. His voice so antiqued, sounding much more like talking, but solid and meant for one woman. Goodmomma would gaze off toward the floor with her hand on his blue pants, every once in a while, smiling to herself, lost in a sea of melody and memory. It was a concert for the family that I grew weary of after so many years but miss more than ever now. Now Gooddaddy sings alone, off into some secluded space where in his mind's eye a white-haired old lady, dressed in purple is seated next to him with her hand on his leg.

<u>Kevin Michael Seder</u>
GoodMama

I was a junior at South Gwinnett High School when GoodMama passed. I was young and my memories are from way after GoodDaddy and GoodMama's medical missionary days, but I still have many great memories and stories I have collected in my mind about our amazing grandparents. I vaguely remember the house they had in Mississippi where the crickets and frogs were so loud, I imagined them as giant creatures hiding in the grass outside our room. I am always reminded by family of the story where I fell in the pond outside of that home while I was squatting down trying to spot fish. GoodDaddy jumped in the pond and pulled me out of the water. I was so young when this happened, I'm not sure if I remember this happening or if I have heard it so many times it feels like I have a picture of it in my mind.

After they moved from Mississippi, GoodMama and GoodDaddy moved to Cartersville, Georgia, into what I believe was a senior community. This was a fun period of time. When my siblings and I would stay over, our daily schedule would begin with waking up whenever we felt like it. Then, GoodMama would ask us what we wanted for breakfast and of course I wanted ice cream with chocolate sauce. Never in my dreams could I have had this at my house, but GoodMama was happy to allow it! As we ate our ice cream we would all watch *Tom & Jerry* cartoons since GoodMama told us it was her favorite show. After our unhealthy breakfast, we would head to the neighborhood pool. GoodMama was a rebel as she would let all of the kids sit on the hood of their big brown Cadillac, we would grab the hood ornament as she slowly made her way the short drive to the pool.

There are many more fun memories I could share, but ultimately, GoodMama left a legacy to her family teaching us how to love God and love others without the pressure to be perfect. She would drop the occasional curse word just to get our attention, she was edgy, fun, caring, adventurous, and lived a life that made an impact on everyone she met.

Chad Alexander Seder
MY GOODMAMA

My GoodMama's life was a shining example on how to serve God, a spouse, family, and people. As I grew up from a child to a teen, my family told me about her work as a nurse, missionary in Africa, loving mother, and wife of fifty-eight years. She lived an extraordinary life and made a difference in everyone's life she encountered. I miss her every day.

Numbers 15 and 17, Chad Seder and Caroline Walker.

A Letter from a Loving Granddaughter

October 5, 2006
Dear GoodMama,

Wow, I can't believe that this is happening. I never thought that I would do something this crazy as to write a letter like this, but the thoughts are just bubbling up inside of me and I'm afraid that I'll go mad if I don't let them out. This has been the hardest thing that I've gone through.

I guess the worst part of it all was the beginning, when I first found out about all of this several months ago. The worst part wasn't the shock. It was the anger, the anger at God that was eating at me from the inside out. I stopped praying, I couldn't anymore and every time that I didn't the worst I felt and the angrier I got. I was so sure that I did something wrong, maybe I wasn't a good enough person.

Then it hit me, it wasn't about me or something I had done, and every time I thought this, I felt myself move further and further away from myself and to the one who is more important than myself, God. So I decided to make a deal with God, silly as it sounds, that if He would give you back to me, we could call it even. I always hated it when people said that to me. It just didn't seem fair that I had all those friends that would give their life just so I could have you back and the one who actually had the power said no. It was made completely obvious to me then that this was not about me.

I love you more than I could or can ever tell you, or perhaps even show you. I'm not going to fill this with "I'm sorry's" and how much I wish I had spent more time with you which is of course where my mind went after the anger faded, and I forgave myself for you being sick. I realized what a waste it would be if I lost my faith because of something as trivial as death. It is trivial, at least in the long run. How could I lose myself and everything that I am over the loss of someone who spent so much of their life in joy, celebrating their faith? I knew then that it was time to get over the anger and the guilt and to move on to the only one true emotion that mattered: love.

So that's what I wanted to tell you. I'm not angry anymore. I'm not guilt-ridden anymore. I gave it all up to the ONE who is greater than all of this and can handle it. In exchange, He filled me up with love. Yes, I'll miss you, so much my heart will ache, but I have love, and I know that when you're gone, you'll be up there, waiting for all of us, and waiting to welcome us with open arms and kisses, and most important, love.

That is what really matters. You will always be in my heart and my mind, so when I get lost, and I will, you can bet on that, I'll have some guidance from someone who has a one-on-one connection with God, YOU.

I love you.

Amy Elrod Fairchild

I learned so many things from GoodMama, who was one of the most amazing women I've ever met. I am the oldest granddaughter, and she always called me her "number 1 Granddaughter." She always made each of us feel so special and loved. Spending weeks in Mississippi at their lake house were full of so many memories, fun and lessons. She taught me to love to read and gave me so many books over the years. Whether she was lying on the couch or sitting on the dock while GoodDaddy was fishing, she always had a book with her. GoodMama taught me the importance of rest—siesta was a part of every afternoon and I actually learned to tell time so I could know what time to get up. She taught me how to play Canasta and I remember hours spent around the table at their Mississippi house playing Canasta. We have carried that tradition on in our family and always think of GoodMama when we play. She taught me so much about cooking—frying fish, making pimento cheese sandwiches, and "grab it and growl meals" when she announced the kitchen was closed and we had to fend for ourselves. GoodMama never met a stranger and was someone everyone loved to be around. GoodMama taught me how to cross-stitch, to play Bingo (and how to win money!) and how to enjoy life. One Christmas she was at our house and woke Ricky and me up at 5:00 a.m. on Christmas morning (isn't it supposed to be the kids that wake up early?). GoodMama showed me the value of a handwritten note—she wrote so many letters to us (many times it was just about what she did that day and I confess I couldn't always read her handwriting). She wrote down quotes to share with people, checked new recipes to try (we found hundreds of recipes checked in her old cookbooks… I don't know how many she actually tried :)) She was so proud of me when I decided to become a nurse and it was so special to be able to share that with her. She showed me how to follow the Lord and your husband as she went back to Africa in the eighties and then moved to the "jungle" of Mississippi. She showed me how to have a love for travel (that my parents multiplied), and when I moved to Brazil as a missionary, I felt like I was following in her footsteps. I am so thankful for the legacy that she and GoodDaddy left for our family. GoodMama always said, "You have to bloom where you are planted," and she lived this every day, whether she was in Africa, Mississippi, or Cartersville. I was there when she found out about her cancer diagnosis and the first words out of her mouth were "Well, you have to bloom where you are planted." In life and even in death she was full of the joy of the Lord. I want to be like GoodMama and live each day to the fullest. I want to enjoy life and find ways to laugh even in the hard times. I want to take time to rest, to spend time with those I love, to have fun and to leave people better off whether they spent five minutes or five hours with me.

<u>James Richard Elrod</u>
"Ricky"

GoodMomma memories… There are so many it's hard to choose, I'll give you some quick ones:

I'll never forget playing Canasta with GoodMomma and GoodDaddy in Silver Run during summer trips I spent with them. GoodMomma would always buy me special food and snacks to eat during our trips. She treated me the way any grandkid would love to be treated—spoiled.

I learned how to tell time because she would make us "rest" while we were in Mississippi. She and GoodDaddy would take a nap and I would have to watch for the clock to line up just right so I knew when I could come out of my room.

I remember her cuss jar :)… Enough said.

I remember her joy and kind spirit. She would do anything for anyone and could talk to anyone.

Leah Page Andrews
Memories of GoodMama

When I think about GoodMama, I can't help but smile. She had the best sense of humor and a contagious grin. I have been blessed to favor GoodMama, and I like to think that I inherited my smile from her. I think my favorite memories of GoodMama are probably visiting GoodDaddy and her at Silver Run in Mississippi. They always made it so fun for us, and we had roads there named after us. No matter where we were, we always had fun when GoodMama was around.

Donald "Walker" Page
Reflection

When I think of GoodMama and GoodDaddy, I am taken back to the living room of the small, one-bedroom flat where they lived their final days together.

GoodMama is sitting in a chair with her embroidery hoop, patiently stitching a beautiful piece to give to someone. GoodDaddy is sitting on the sofa, resting with his hands folded and eyes closed. "Unforgettable" by Nat King Cole is playing in the background. What stands out to me is how they lived with a kind of simplicity and quiet stillness—traits which are not surprising to see in former missionaries to Africa. Their lives manifested the Lord's command to "Be still, and know that I am God" (Psalm 46:10—one of GoodMama's favorite verses). Although I remember them living a simple life, I remember it also as a rich one, full of love and relationships. As they sit in that living room, I see them not alone, but surrounded by pictures of their many children, grandchildren, and great-grandchildren. I see joy fill their faces as they look up and scan those pictures. But their deepest love and joy is revealed as they turn to one another and see the one whom their soul loves.

Lessons from Other Mothers

M y question for friends: What is a lesson your mother taught you and how have you applied it in your life?

I am grateful for each remarkable response that follows:

From Charlotte B.

My mama fought the good fight, finished the race, and went onto receive her eternal rewards on February 9, 2018. A woman who loved her family fiercely and an inspiration to all who knew her. I was always so proud to be her "baby." Mama had me as a planned fourth child at age forty, and she never cared about her age. Mama feared God, not man. She was a friend to many, a helper of the helpless, an encourager for the wayward, had a great style without a love of a mirror, and lived in complete confidence in who God made her to be. Mama always encouraged us to do the same. A career as a high school history teacher, Mama taught with her whole heart. Our family was blessed by her gift of a godly wife, mother, hospitable homemaker and so much more. Thank you, Mama. What a grand ninety-seven years!

From Jan P.

Live each moment, easy or hard, good or bad.

One of the most precious lessons learned from my momma occurred while watching her manage the passing of my dad. At the time, little did I know I would travel the same journey.

A little bit about my momma…she loved large and unconditionally, was giving, positive, upbeat, fun, and a woman of faith. She and Dad had a very loving relationship, focusing on my brother and I, and building a home filled with love and laughter.

My dad was a very loving, strong, healthy man that could do anything. When the news came that he had lung cancer it was surprising and devastating. Dad's cancer was advanced and he was not given a good prognosis. I watched my mother grieve and then quickly migrate into a full-out mode of a loving, supportive, nurturing, positive partner. Mom and Dad leaned on each other and lived each day as positive as possible. On difficult days they would count their many blessings and lean on the Lord. During this journey Dad's faith became deeper and he accepted the mighty Father into his heart. They demonstrated strength that was truly an inspiration to many.

Seventeen years later, I would find myself in the same situation, my loving husband would be diagnosed with lung cancer. During our journey my prayer many times was for the strength and grace that my Momma displayed. Together Chris and I, our children, and many loved ones shared special moments and made many memories that will be forever cherished. Chris had the Lord in his heart and was prepared to meet the Father. His passing was difficult, but I'm blessed to have had a love so special.

As we each go through life, days will be made up of good, bad, easy, and hard moments/hours. Cherish every day as there are no "redos."

From Brenda P.

Like most Southern moms, my mama could come up with some zingers!

She was content as a homemaker when I was a young child and then decided to follow her talents and rejoin the work force as a top-notch executive secretary.

Over the years, she would say, "You can catch more flies with honey." Her interpretation of that was when you deal with frustrating situations or people (flies are annoying, right?!), it is easier to resolve disputes and draw people over to your side by being "sweeter" (honey), kinder, more polite. Think customer no service situations!

Mama would also say, "Stay calm, cool, and collected." In my earlier years, my Irish genes found my Mom's sentiments to be very challenging. I actually enjoyed "chewing people out," when I knew I was right and they were wrong. But with the wisdom that older age brings, I find that when you are the one that lashes out and loses your temper, you end up apologizing for your behavior.

So take my Mama's advice and take the high road. Listen more, talk less. You'll be surprised how much lower your blood pressure is!

From Molly B.

Always write a nice thank-you note!

My mother was adamant about this, and it had to be sincere and descriptive. I can remember her being upset if she didn't receive a thank you note after she gave a gift. My biggest challenge at writing notes was for our wedding gifts. I still easily recall how agonizing it was to write so many notes!

I've applied this lesson to this day in my life and I also instilled the same lesson in our daughter. As a child, I wouldn't let her play with gifts until she wrote a note of thanks. It was harsh, perhaps, but it proved an important point. To this day, she writes nice thank you notes, although I don't think she keeps gifts from her children until they write theirs…perhaps I was too strict!

Taking the time and effort to send a handwritten note is a joy to the one receiving it!

From Susanna H.

When I think of my Mother, the following Bible scripture comes into my mind:

> "Be ye steadfast, immovable, always abounding in the work of The Lord, knowing that your labor is not in vain."

> 1 Corinthians 15:58

My mother truly portrayed steadfast commitment toward her God and toward her family. Her example gave me confidence and trust in God Almighty and in His Son, The Lord Jesus Christ. It has encouraged me to desire a life of daily walking with The Lord, as I serve my own family.

What wonderful blessings God brings to me as I walk through life with Him and live in His active presence.

From Debbie W.

A Lesson from My Mom

Because of Dad's job, we moved often. When I was engaged, I asked my mother how she seemed so cheerful even though they were moving yet again. Mom smiled and said, "God showed me that I could be miserable whenever we moved, *or* I could appreciate my new home and joyfully jump into new experiences like Women's Bible Studies, help in the church Sunday School Department, help your father with the youth group, and getting to know our new neighbors." Mom lived this, and they have friends all over the country.

At the time, I was engaged to John, who intended to go to medical school and would be in ROTC. Later, he would obtain an air force scholarship to attend medical school. This plan meant that we, too, would be moving fairly often. (I moved nine times as a child and have moved ten times since marriage.) I wholeheartedly embraced my mother's keen advice. It wasn't always easy, but it was a blessing. We look back and see God's hand in all of it. We, too, are blessed with friends across the country. Friends who are still very much a part of our lives, who have prayed for us, given us wisdom that only godly friends can and who love us well. I am so very thankful for a mom and dad who showed me how to love Jesus.

From Kelly H.

Never give up on your dream.

My mother first dreamed of writing a book in her high school and college years, although never thought it possible. As a child, she remembered making up stories and playing with imaginary friends. Imagination has always been her strength. Through the years, she wrote bits of poetry and kept notes on conversations and quirky characteristics observed in others. Mother kept these notes in her own filing cabinet, separate from my father's financial and home records. Her poetry always rhymed and was usually funny; and her story ideas eventually became novels.

Although I never knew until I had children of my own, Mother had been working on a novel for many years. When I was a child, she made notes on her notepad, after work in the evenings, and may have written after putting me to bed. After retiring from dental hygiene in her fifties, Mother attended numerous writing conferences and pitched her book proposal to traditional publishers. Several liked her idea, but none offered a contract.

At age sixty, discouraged with the publishing industry and almost ready to quit, Mother finished her first novel. A love story set during World War II (her passion), she self-published it a few years later, at the age of sixty-three. She then set to work on her second novel, also a romance set during WWII, and self-published it at age seventy-six.

It was anything but easy. Despite an aversion to computers, Mother overcame the challenge. With tech assistance from my husband and the application of her excellent typing skills, she got her book into Microsoft Word. Mother overcame technology, the challenges of a well-meaning yet exacting husband, and the tightly locked doors of the traditional publishing industry. Through tears, setbacks, and various obstacles, her determination kept her going. She did it. Mother followed her passion, her dream, and her heart's desire all the way to completion and, in the process, inspired me to do the same.

From Karen W.

There are two ways to approach "chores" in life. One way is to dread them, and another is to consider them a way to nurture your loved ones. Momma lived this out by example as she always approached cooking and providing for us as pure pleasure. Momma came from a small town, Helen, Georgia and as a young girl she dreamed of seeing the big, wide world. After marrying Daddy, they found themselves with great opportunities to travel. Daddy, a clinical psychologist, was a behavior modification researcher in London for close to a year when my brother, sister, and I were young. Momma never considered it a burden to travel with her family of five. Instead, she always regarded traveling the world as an adventure.

From Sandy G.

My Momma passed away on December 18, 2010, at the young age of sixty-one. Momma suffered from a disease called alcoholism. Trouble stemming from her disease came and went through the years. She was able to live with our family steadily and alcohol-free from 1997 through 2005. The children, my husband, and I enjoyed her immensely in the course of those love-filled years.

One of the many things Momma taught me was how to be a loving grandmother. And thank goodness she did! We have four children and so far, two granddaughters to celebrate life with. A little brother will join his two sisters in early August 2021. Momma taught me through her actions and words to have two ready hands to help out when a household was a busy one like my daughter's.

Even though I had to say "See you later, Momma," too soon, I am so grateful for all the things that she taught me. In 2005, Momma returned to North Carolina to take care of my Granny. The truth is that sadly, her addiction called her away. When Granny passed on in 2009, her addiction picked up speed. During one of her binges, in the summer of 2010 she fell, breaking her hip, and needing great care. We were able to bring Momma back to Georgia before she passed on later that year. I know I will see Momma again, and there will be rejoicing when we do. There will be no more tears and no more disease. I love you, Momma.

From Rita M.

So many memories flood into my mind when I consider lessons my Mom taught me. Family always came first. Mom was one of six, so aunts, uncles, and grands were always around during the week-ends. They were their "base" of friends. "Always trust your gut." As the baby, I heard this spoken often to my older sisters and brother. This was cemented into my head to always go with your gut feelings. Mom continually reminded us that we were responsible for our own faith, making sure we attended church regularly. Mom had the sweetest personality and was loved by all who knew her. I especially remember this during her later years when Mom lived in a nursing home. As a child, it is easy for me to recall Mom's happy and positive demeanor, always singing or humming. Mom loved music. Even today, when I hear a song that she sang, I picture her in our kitchen, cooking and singing, and this warms my heart. This is a memory that will stay with me forever.

From Donna K.

Words of Wisdom from my mother: There with the grace of God go I.

(Everything in your life is a gift from God.)

To whom much is given, much is expected.

(God has given you much, worship Him and honor Him in all you do with those gifts. Work hard and give to those in need. Make a difference for Him.)

You can do anything you put your mind to.

Rise above it, honey!

The Good Lord has been so, so good to us all our lives (when referring to serious challenges and hardships in our family).

Offer it up!

From Jan C.

I have three lessons from my Mama and each one is very different!

1.   Always wear clean underwear (smile).
2.   Always be kind and respectful.
3.   Have a cocktail or other refreshing beverage at five o'clock to make cooking dinner more enjoyable.

And one lesson I have shared with our two children through the years: Put down cell phones and technology to enjoy all who are around you and to better hear the littles who are in your home.

From Debby B.

One of the most important lessons I learned from my mother was to give fully of my time and talents to others. My mother never had a paid job after her first child was born, but she was busier and worked harder than any other mom I knew. She was a great organizer, and so served as an officer in almost every school and community organization that was available. She helped organize a local children's theater and spent years using her sewing talents to make too many costumes to count. She volunteered for numerous charitable organizations and for years, organized ticket sales, and volunteer ushers for the Broadway Theater League.

Although I have worked full time as a high school teacher all of my adult life, I have found myself volunteering and serving in many of these same ways. I volunteer for many missions activities and have served as an officer in many committees at my church. For years, I assisted as the director of my school's drama program. My mother taught me to sew when I was in elementary school and I found myself sewing countless costumes, just like my mother! Since the pandemic began, I have sewn and donated over 150 masks to a variety of groups in our community. Just like my mother, I consider it a privilege to use my skills and talents to help others.

From Cindy A.

One of the most important things I learned from my sweet Mom was to be involved in the lives of others. Mom taught us this by example. Here's how. A mother to four and wife to a busy husband who traveled a lot, Mom decided to go back to college to become a teacher. Even amidst a busy schedule, we always had a home cooked meal and time with her every day. While I don't remember her studying, as a straight-A student, I know she did. She must have done so after we were all tucked into bed.

My mom was one of the few mothers I knew that worked outside the home. She still managed to be very involved in everything we did and was such a great role model for us all. It was obvious her students loved Mom, and she cared deeply about her students. She would even go to their extra-curricular activities to support them. I believe many of her students had difficult home situations. Mom became a safe person for them. She would listen and make them feel important and valued.

Later, Mom went back to school to get her Masters-in-Counseling. This was an ideal field for her as she was already doing so much counseling as a teacher. By this time, the four of us were teenagers. Mom remained very engaged with all of our activities, even serving as advisor for our high school sorority. I just took it for granted! Now that I am a Mom myself, I do not know how she did all that she did with such grace. Mom never missed a thing. She continues to be present in all of our lives as a mom, a grandmother, great-grandmother, and a devoted friend.

When Mom is with you, she is focused on you and only you. I try to remember to do the same, however I am not always successful. I trust that my children and grandchildren see that I am present and living out the moments with them, day by day, just like my mom did.

From Laura A.

My mom was not one to advise her kids with pearls of wisdom, that was my dad's area, but she did teach us, nevertheless. She continues to teach me daily. It's my parents' voices that I hear in my head when making decisions. Mom taught me by example by living a compassionate and inclusive life. Her children were challenges, by her generation's viewpoint. However, Mom made sure that we never felt like the "challenges" that society would judge us by. "Live and let live" was a sentiment that I often heard from her. She kept a Buddha in her garden, a mezuzah by the entrance to her home, and a cross over her bed. She believed each one represented a religion with lessons to live by. I thank the Lord, Buddha, Jesus, Allah, or whomever or whatever, that I had to the good fortune of being her daughter.

Because of my Mom's faith in me, I think I have more faith in the people in my life. And one more lesson I learned from my mom…is that although shaming someone may get you what you want in the short run, it never helps in the long run.

From Jane Ellen B.

Probably the best and most important lesson that mom ever taught me I really just learned by example. It wasn't anything that she necessarily said, but the way she lives her life. Mom is always, I mean in every single situation thinking of others before herself. Sometimes, I have to admit it doesn't sit well with me, but nevertheless the lesson is there. Mom constantly wants to make others happy. Her middle name is "go"! I don't think that I've ever asked her to do something that she has said no to. She has even been known to break a doctor's appointment opting out for something more fun. I would say that she is the go-to person that everyone calls on because she is always more than willing to be there for others whether it is in time of celebration, sorrow, or just plain old friendship. Like I said before, sometimes it doesn't sit well with me… I just wish that sometimes when she needs an extra hand that she would let others help her as well. She is now eighty-seven and still goes the extra mile for everyone, never complaining about her aches and pains, she is amazing! I could site so many examples, but then I'd have to write a book!

From Susan Brown

As one of six, three sisters and three brothers, I felt compelled to brainstorm with my siblings for input on Lessons from our Mom.

Here we go!

"When you pray and ask the Lord for something, you have to give Him time to work. Don't run ahead of Him. Wait and be patient. He always answers." This has been a constant reminder to me in my prayer life. God is not on our timetable. Be quiet and watchful.

"Be content with what you have and where you are!" When I taught at Mount Paran Christian School and saw the lifestyles many led (not teachers:)) I would get caught up with wanting more. I would go visit my mom and one time I wanted to take her shopping for new black shoes. Her comment: "I already have two pairs, why would I need another?" It stopped me in my tracks and made me rethink. I swallowed "a contentment pill" and was thankful for the restart!

"Have a servant's heart with your career and finances." This is from my sister, Linda who is a retired nurse. I have observed her natural ability to be a caretaker with our family and community members for decades. This is her special way to serve Him. Linda loves big and always shares her time, talent, and treasures.

"Don't get bossy with older folks!" This is from my brother, David. HaHa! His application is, "Don't mess with me as I grow old."

We have all watched our sweet Mom of ninety years old, still of an incredibly sound mind, be in charge and make decisions. Mom gives God time to work and won't be bullied by her six grown kids into hurrying up to act immediately. Mom lives alone and has now become a caregiver for her ninety-seven-year-old blind sister. Mom is not in fantastic health herself, but she will continue on to always think of others.

I could go on and on with many more lessons I learned from my dear Mom, but I will end with this one:

"Appreciate a man that hears an alarm in the morning and gets up to go to work to provide for his family."

From Delores

My lesson would probably go along with your lesson 8…Give your children roots and wings. At an early age, I can always remember Mom teaching me about the importance of family—doing things with family, sticking by them through whatever may happen, working through your problems together. Mom also taught me the importance of independence and being able to stand on my own two feet. She was always very encouraging in wanting me to get out on my own and live before settling down to a new family of my own.

At a young age, I can remember pushing a chair up to the kitchen counter and standing on it. Here, Mom would teach me to cook. I was a seventh or eighth grader at this time and Mom had started working a new job. I was proudly preparing most of our meals!

Mom taught me about a checking account and how to keep track of your money. I learned the importance of not overspending your means and the importance of saving for "a rainy day." By the time I graduated from high school, I knew I could live on my own. I just needed more education!

I have always been so appreciative of all these life lessons.

From Evelyn W.

My mom has some "lesson worthy" quotes, like "just because everyone else is doing it doesn't mean it's okay for you to do it." Of course, at the time I interpreted this as some sort of punishment. What she really taught me was *independence.*

Another of her favorite quotes is "I learned that when I was in the army." My mom was never in the army, but what I realized later is that many of life's lessons are just that—taken from life experiences, while in the trenches of living.

From Lynn B.

My mama taught me lots of lessons…the way she taught wasn't necessarily sitting us down and talking to us. Our Dad was the one that would patiently teach us how to do tasks, learn new things and help with school projects. The way Mom "taught" us was by the way she lived every day. She lived with *faith*!

Mom went through a lot in her life…finding out that her oldest son was gay, losing a son at the young age of twenty to a moped accident on the first day of our family vacation in the Cayman Islands, and then, two months later hearing that your eldest son has tested positive for HIV. Living with cancer for nearly two decades, enduring some pretty tough treatments and *rarely* complaining, along with other traumatic life experiences.

Mom strived to keep things normal, soldiering on, in spite of all the adversity. She was positive, fun-loving, active, hardworking, and adored by a multitude of friends of all ages!

Despite the fact that she weathered so much throughout her life,

It always amazed me how she could go to bed and actually *sleep* every night. Getting on her knees, giving it to God and simply *know*

He was in control. Anytime I was going through a trial, she would remind me that "worrying will do nothing."

"In all thy ways acknowledge Him and he
shall direct thy Paths."

Proverbs 3:6

I have to admit I don't do this near as well as she did, but I did learn without a doubt that HE is in *control*...and even though it may not be in My timing, I do know to *give* it to HIM and HE *will* direct my path.

I miss my *mom* every day!

She was my biggest cheerleader as well as my best friend. I will never be able to name all of the lessons she taught me. Mostly to love life, to be grateful for what we have, and to always remember who is in control. She was a pillar of strength for many and the loving backbone of our family!

Kelly R.

In honor of my "Mama."

Mary Margaret "Peggy" Curphey, fondly referred to as everyone's "Mimi!"

"Everything happens for a reason...give it time."

A "tried but true" lesson from my mother, often described as the "strongest and classiest lady I know" by my many friends who are blessed to "know her." Our quick response to these words of "reassurance" in times of trouble, sadness, confusion, or grief is often "no, it doesn't"...no reason could be worth my overwhelming sense of trouble, sadness, confusion, or grief at this moment in my life. But wait, did you hear the next three words in this lesson... *"give it time?"* This is where the "reassurance" comes in...would we change what has happened in our lives that causes us such great sadness; of course, but can we? No...this chapter in our life journey is now a reality. So what are we to do? We *"give it time"* and then one day we start to see the unforeseeable blessings unfold that begin to heal our hearts and souls. "Mimi" will also tell you to be patient and open to watching for these blessings…they may appear in days, weeks, months, or years to come but they "will come." Be it in the smallest of events or moments that cause you to feel the slightest bit of joy again or a life-changing, beautiful experience that brings happiness to many lives as well as your own. All of this because of the chapter in your life journey. So the next time someone shares these words of reassurance "Everything happens for a reason"…remember my mother's next three words and be reassured *"give it time"* and watch as beautiful blessings both large and small unfold in your life and those you love.

From Leah A.

Lessons from My Mom

There are so many things I've learned from my mom, and I realize them more and more as I've grown older. I'm going to share two that specifically come to mind.

One thing I have learned from my mom is how to be truly selfless. Throughout my life if there is one quality about my Mom, I have always admired it's her selflessness. My mom goes above and beyond to help others. She gave up her career to stay at home and raise my brother and me. She is constantly putting her family, friends and really everyone's needs before her own. She thinks of others consistently and how she can help people. I strive to be selfless like her in my life.

Another thing I learned from my mom that I try to practice in my life is what she calls the "sandwich method." Whenever you must deliver any kind of bad, negative, or disappointing news to someone, she says to use the sandwich method. Start by telling them something positive, then bring up the negative, and then end with a positive. I have used this in my life, and I have found that it is so helpful. People are receptive to this method and accepting of the negative when it's surrounded by positive.

From Donalee

A mother's love is precious. I know it is true because of what Mama's love has expressed to me. Precious is the "bestest" way to describe it. It has helped me begin to comprehend the Heavenly Father's love for me for which I am most grateful. This must be stated first because only in grasping God's love can we truly love others. My mama's love taught me there is no higher calling for me than to be a mother and for a lifetime. I remember being asked time and again as a child "what do you want to be when you grow up?" My dream occupations ranged from nurse, to veterinarian, to circus lady, to archaeologist, and so on. But the longing of my heart was to be a mom. It was constant and kept growing deeper and stronger as I matured.

Mama birthed me at the age of twenty. It was the year after she married Daddy and they moved from Boston to Northern Maine. I was her first born and became her little helper over the years as four more babies came along. I played dollies a long while and loved pretending I was a mommy as I observed her as a homemaker and mother of five. Mama did mentor me in many of the skills helpful to have experience/understanding for running a home and raise a family and I am thankful of this. But what she taught me in being a mother that matters most is Faith in God Almighty, Hope for eternity through Jesus Christ, and the greatest of all Love...and for one another. Thanks, Mama.

"With my mouth will I make known Your faithfulness to all generations."

Psalm 89:1

"This is my command that you love one another as I have loved you."

John 15:12

From Sara R. S.

One of many lessons I have learned from my Mom is persever-ance. At twenty-four years of age and newly wedded, both Momma and Daddy were overjoyed to find out they were expecting their first child. My brother, Jay was born September 9, 1956. The doctors were solemn as they came in and announced to my parents that Jay had Down's Syndrome. The doctors said that Jay most likely would not live past the age of twelve. He would not smile or be a viable member of our family. My parents were crushed and wrestled with what to do. After many tears and much prayer, they decided to take Jay home and love him with faith that God would provide. And He did!

Momma and Daddy persevered. They loved Jay, encouraged Jay, educated Jay, and involved him in all that his two sisters had going on. He walked, smiled beautifully, and joyfully, was in Special Olympics during the summers, was on a bowling team, and was very much involved in Civitan.

At the age of sixty-four, our brother, Jay went home to be with the Lord on December 11, 2020. Jay was such a blessing to our fam-ily and a true asset to my life. Watching my Mom, I have learned about perseverance in the unknown and faith that God has a beauti-ful purpose in all things. Momma has shown me that God will pro-vide what is needed to accomplish His purposes…one day at a time.

From Martha B.

Momma taught my five sisters and me that we are to minister, being the hands and feet of Jesus until we leave this earth. Momma's service was never flashy. Often behind the scenes and never men-tioned. I learned about many of her ministries when I was an adult and even after her passing. Momma taught Sunday school to a group of ladies as far back as I can recall. Until she moved to an assisted living facility and could no longer drive. Even then, Momma helped lead/care for a Bible study in this new home of hers. "Martha, God did not mention the word 'retire' in the Bible," she would often say. Sometimes, we would come to her room on Sunday mornings telling her that we were too tired to attend church because we were out late the night before.

Her reply was always the same: "If you are too tired to go to church, you are more tired than the Lord intended."

We went to church.

From Meleah

As the middle child of five, I had a unique perspective of our family life. Two boys were born before me. Soon came another brother and a little sister as the caboose. There were many mouths to feed, and it seemed like Mom was forever in the kitchen. Dad was unfailingly busy with work. Therefore, Mom had the five of us in the forefront of her mind. Like Mom, I have always enjoyed putting our family first, as well, no matter what.

Mom needed my help with baths and care for my two younger siblings. I was always willing to help.

I know, for sure, that the time I spent helping with the two of them contributed to my skills when I became a Mom to two little boys. However, the greatest thing my Mom gave me that I have passed on to my own family is the gift of unconditional love.

Mom was an identical twin and as we were growing up. My Aunt Margie was like having a second Mom. When I was thirty-nine and my Mom was only sixty-six years of age, a cancer diagnosis took her from us six months later. I know Mom would have so loved being a great-grandmother to nearly a dozen littles, including our four grandsons!

From Treva Shivers Graham (my first cousin)
pictured here with her Aunt Polly.

My precious mother, Charleen Elizabeth Shivers, went to Heaven fifty years ago in 1971 when she was forty-eight and I was seventeen. I was a senior in high school. She was truly a Proverbs 31 woman, a pastor's wife and a mother of five children, four boys and me. She was beautiful and loved. She cared for her family even when she was suffering with pain. Every time I hear the hymn "Blessed Be the Name of the Lord" I think of the Sunday mornings when I sat beside my mother in church and sang this hymn with her. She was a wonderful homemaker and enjoyed welcoming guests to share a meal with our family. She worked hard, was patient, loved others and lived her life with grace. I learned many things from my mother, and I am so thankful for so many precious memories.

From Lynne

My mom "always" sat down with me in times of trouble and sadness! I would remember her telling me "This, too, shall pass." Sometimes, it seemed long before "it" would actually pass, and Mom would say, "Keep Praying." I still, to this day, hold close to these wise words and wisdom.

From Beth A.

I grew up with a casserole on my lap and my grandmother's roses in a vase between my feet, while my mother drove to someone's house in Greene County, Tennessee. All I knew was somebody had died, had a baby, or was sick. This errand was never optional, and the lesson wasn't optional either. My mother is ninety-two. I have people to this day tell me they remember what we brought to their family. She taught me that giving to others is simply a way of life.

While my mother taught me too many things to include here, I must add her consistent response when life got difficult: "There's nothing you can't get through if you have the Lord with you."

From Melissa W.

> My mom's favorite Bible verse is "This is the day the Lord has made let us rejoice and be glad in it!."
>
> Psalm 118:24

This is my prayer each morning as I start my day! My mom taught me to love well! It actually makes me cry to think of how much my mother loves our family and friends! She is a true example of loving her Lord and loving others. She always puts others above herself and is generous and thoughtful with her time.

She and my dad were always present for all of our daily activities and events and walked along side us. She has always encouraged time with family and is intentional to stay in touch with family and stressed the importance of family time. She also encouraged me to give back and support our friends, neighbors, church, school, and community.

> "Do small things with great love."
>
> Mother Teresa

Her examples have encouraged me and my sister to continue these traditions in our family. A wonderful legacy.

From Allison H.

You have to know when it's good enough.

"You have to know when it is good enough," my mother said to me. She spoke these guiding words gently, and often. My mother recognized my struggles with perfectionism early on. How she didn't rip her lovely red hair out, I do not know. I gave her reasons, so many reasons. I think I've lost some of my own hair just thinking about it.

"You have to know when it's good enough if you want to accomplish anything." She would tell me, "Done is better than perfect." My mom learned this lesson years ago after she and my father divorced. She was a newly single mother with three teenage kids who had college aspirations. She was fortunate to have success modeled for her by my grandfather, who was a sought-after veterinarian and shrewd businessman. *Live below your means* was his motto and he and my grandmother lived that motto out daily.

My mother landed an excellent job around that time, as the president of our local chamber of commerce. She had a college degree, was a teacher for some time and worked various jobs during our early years. Someone recommended her for the chamber job based on the way she occupied space in the world. She was smart, positive, kept a level head, and had an uncommon ability to roll with the punches. She had no chamber of commerce experience, but they took a chance on her. She was entrusted to write her own job description and she knew it was an answer to prayer.

My mother was fortunate to have excellent mentors on her board of directors. They were supportive; yet challenging. When she brought something to them, whether an idea or a concern, they listened, asked her questions, and gave her room to grow. They were not interested in her perfection, rather her growth and ability to move forward without all the answers. During one of my phone calls pleading for her help with my perfectionistic tendencies, she shared that a board member told her one of his secrets to success, "You have to know when something is good enough." and "Done is better than perfect," he told her. If she was going to make an impact in a brand-new position, she was going to have to get things done! She knew she had to prove herself, and fast. She would have to make decisions and take chances. Perfect doesn't matter if it never makes it out of your head and into the world.

Moving forward with something that is less than perfect is tough for a recovering perfectionist such as myself, but this advice has really helped me grow over the years. As a mother of three, I spent my years trying to make things perfect for everyone—an impossibility for sure—and as a writer, who wants your mistakes inked for all time? I have always admired my mother's ability to take imperfect action. If she committed to something, my brothers and I knew she would make it happen or give it everything she had trying. It was never about a perfect plan; it was about the beautiful journey unfolding amidst the imperfect plan.

I have asked myself many times, why would I chase the impossible? I don't have an answer yet, but I am learning to move beyond that limiting attitude and make progress. Perfect is paralyzing and I have some big goals ahead of me. I am running toward them, and even if I trip and fall, I will keep moving. Besides, I think battle scars are cool. They say, "Hey, there's someone who's been through some stuff and survived. That person has wisdom to share."

Where is the adventure in a perfect plan, perfectly executed anyway? What stories would I have to tell that anyone would want to read? The unexpected holds so much wonder, so many opportunities to love, to flow, and to grow. I am showing up perfectly imperfect, taking messy action and getting things done. The journey requires courage, humility, and a savvy redhead named Ruthie. I am blessed to call her mom.

From Cyndi W.

My mom taught me how to listen. Listening can seem to be somewhat of a lost art with the busyness and noise in our world today. In my world, growing up, my Mom always seemed to find the time to listen. We often had guests at our house. Some of them were front door guests, but most of them were friends and neighbors who came in the back door, unannounced and knowing they were always welcome, regardless of the cleanliness of our home. Most of the conversations were around the kitchen table with a cup of coffee or outside on pretty Georgia days with a cool drink. Somewhere, along the way in my growing up, I realized in my comings and goings during these conversations, that my Mom didn't do much of the talking. Instead, she listened…to worries and fears and frustrations and confidences and tears of both joy and sadness. And when she did speak, her words were without judgment and were filled with encouragement, grace, hope, and truth in love. Listening was her gift, taking the time to hear from the soul deep hearts of others. Whether they were the dearest of friends or those who were isolated, often misunderstood or considered by many as more of an EGR (extra grace required), she would listen with the same attentiveness and care for all. Mom knew something that I came to understand as an adult, something very valuable and life-giving…the gift of listening. Because in this good, difficult life, we all long to be heard, to know and be known. May it be so in me.

From Debbie P.

While my mother is a good person, I truly don't recall her "pearls of wisdom." Mom worked a lot when I was young.

If anyone helped to form my ideals it would have been my Grandmother, Elizabeth. Grandmama did this mostly by her daily example. Her "can do it" attitude and her hard work ethic definitely made an impact on my life.

In addition, there were also others that helped mold me when I was young, my friends' mothers. All my "Camp Fire Moms" were always there to encourage me, without fail. I know you, Joan, were a Brownie Girl Scout and not a Camp Fire Girl, still, I included your Mom in this group of those who were there for me. She was an amazing person.

From Kay B.

My mother, Grace Green, is the most perfect woman I've ever known. Grace…such a fitting name for my mother, for it describes her perfectly. Mama taught me many positive lessons, mostly by her faithful, consistent actions. She taught and showed me to "Love the Lord thy God with all thy heart, with all thy soul, and with all thy mind." She also modeled unwavering, unconditional love for family and others, as prescribed in Matthew 22:39, "Thou shalt love thy neighbor as thyself."

As I write this, I realize these traits are what Jesus, himself noted as the two greatest commandments.

I come nowhere near measuring up to the example Mama set for me. However, I do have an uncanny ability to love people big. Like her, I do whatever I can to help my family and my friends, often putting their needs and wants above mine. Her examples help me to be loyal, even when it may not be reciprocated. I try to exemplify 1 Corinthians 12:13b, which says, "But the greatest of these is love."

I count it all joy to be the daughter of Grace Green!

From Susan F.

Mom definitely "bloomed where she was planted." Her home-life was full of chaos and she felt little love as she was growing up. The Holy Spirit led Mom to First Baptist Church in Knoxville, Tennessee. Here, she met Jesus and was baptized at nine years old, by herself. Mom was never alone again, and God blessed her life in so many ways. It wasn't easy, but He gave Mom great vision and purpose. Mom taught us about love. Our two big brothers, my twin sister and I always felt loved and cared for. Most importantly, Mom instilled in us the truth about God's love for each one of us.

Mom told us "that she never caught her Mom's love."

She made certain we knew how very loved we were. All four of us caught her love.

From JoAnn

The Value of Family

Mom taught us the value of family. Mom always instilled that family was family no matter what they said or did. She encouraged us to always forgive each other and to pray for our family members. She taught us family loyalty in all matters. Mom reminded us that one day she would be long gone, but our family would always remain.

Fast forward to my life now...family is still very important to me. From Mom's four children, we now have thirty-four in our extended family, with whom I enjoy spending quality time. God has truly blessed each and every one of us.

Please take a long look at your family and think about all the ways they enhance your life.

From Trish O.

As the baby of three sisters, my mother was age twenty-four when I joined the family. There are so many things she instilled in me. I will share a few here. Education was always important! Mum was a teacher and completed her Masters at age thirty. She had such a sense of adventure, and this often spilled out onto our family. Mum encouraged play with my sisters and me. We played house, school, and even church. With the church play, she laughingly said, "Now that's just taking it too far!" Our faith was to be respected and revered. We were taught by example to kneel bedside to pray each night.

A few more important lessons include the following:

Do the right thing the first time.

Have integrity. Do the right thing even when no one is looking.

Look it up! When we had a question, rather than simply giving us the answer, we were taken to the library. We were taught to research to find the answer ourselves. (And this was before Google, lol.)

From Susan B.

Lesson: Only your best friend would tell you that.

This is just one of the lessons from my mom that I have passed on to my children as well. If you were to put it into today's language it would probably be a cross between "I'm just keeping it real" and "you know I have your back."

One of the earliest times I remember this lesson from my Mom was when, as a teenager, I was saying goodbye as I left the house to go out with friends. She stopped me and announced that my blue eyeshadow application made me look like I belonged in a "French whorehouse." Of course, I did not appreciate her honesty, and was both defensive and furious at her comment. She then followed with "only your best friend would tell you that!" Wow! Let that sink in! My mom returned to this lesson many other times through the years. Some were situations like this one, and others, while never life-threatening, were far more significant.

In addition to her fashion commentary, there were times when she called me out because my perspective or attitude toward a situation was just plain wrong. There were also times when she felt that even as an adult, my behavior in a situation or toward someone was inappropriate. Each of these times, she would follow *the blow* with "only your best friend would tell you that." The underlying and unmistakable truth every time was that no matter the message, she was indeed my *best friend*, and she loved me deeply! I knew without question, that her motivation was always her love for me, and her intention was to help, and make me a better person.

I now know of the courage required on her part to speak up in many of those times. None of us likes conflict or confrontation, whether with extended family, friends, or even when "parenting" an adult child. We are all challenged from time to time with situations where our hearts and minds see that things are amiss, yet we find it so difficult to be honest. Regardless of our best intentions, our greatest fear is that we will somehow damage the relationships that matter to us the most. We care for our people so deeply that we are afraid to cause a rift, or worse to lose their trust and love.

I love the fact that my mother felt confident enough in our relationship, that she was willing to share difficult truths with me when I needed to hear them most. The Bible tells us that we are to speak the truth in love: Ephesians 4:15. Truth and love go hand-in-hand. Because we love one another we must always strive to speak the truth, even when it's hard. These are the truths that are beneficial to our loved ones and help build them up. These are the times when "only your best friend would tell you that!"

A Note from Joan

I liken the writing of this book to birthing a baby. The gestation period, however, was way longer than nine months...more like nine years! In 2008, just two years after Mama's homegoing, I began my blog, *Pages From Joan*, in her memory. A short time later, the idea for this book came into my thoughts and planted itself into my heart. Through the years, the idea grew and bloomed. I knew it would come to fruition. I knew in my heart of hearts that it would come to be. Lesson learned: Never give up on a dream.

And speaking of babies, as this work goes to print, our family celebrates the birth of two new grandchildren who just arrived in early September 2021!

I am grateful for you, my reader. Thank you for taking time out to dive into this book of Mama's wisdom with me. Mama loved making notations in books, cookbooks, on the back of photos, and in her well-worn Bible, always dating them as she wrote out her thoughts. My prayer is that this little book will be one you will mark in, highlight quotes in and gain clarity from. Life is short. This is not a dress rehearsal. Let's do this life thing the best that we can, while we still have time.

A true story about the origin of my birth name. I gave up my middle name when I married Donny Page on October 2, 1982. Ironically, I didn't love my given middle name, "Lynelle" until I was all grown and had been married for a few years. You see, it was then that I learned the truth of the origin of my middle name. If you refer back to *My Family Tree* at the beginning of this journey, you will be reminded that Mama's name on her birth certificate was "JoNelle."

My parents decided to use this, creating "Joan Lynelle" for their fourth daughter's name. Don't ask me why I never knew this before. It was likely the lively, bustling seasons of life. Once this was discovered, my birth name was extra special to me! In later years, Mama would come to write the name "Joy" in her notes and letters to me. This, too, brought me happiness as she claimed my life brought her much joy, as did the lives of my three sisters and two brothers, and all of our extended family members.

It would be an impossible task to thank all who have pushed, prompted, and encouraged me in my writing season. There are too many family members and friends to count. So many who have prodded me along to finish this project. You know who you are, and I thank you for believing in me and never giving up on me. I will be forever indebted to all who have prayed fervently for the completion of this project.

I am filled with gratitude for my long-time friend, writer, and blogger of Southern Food and Fun, Rebecca (Lucy) Brewer (www.southernfoodandfun.com). Rebecca lovingly devoted an extraordinary number of hours helping me set up my blog years ago and has been one of my greatest cheerleaders in the writing process.

Both Mindy Kiker and Jenny Kochert, co-founders of Flourish Gathering and Flourish Writers have provided me with so many valuable opportunities to work on my writing craft. Mindy and Jenny are passionate to help writers to grow in God's Word. Together they have authored and published numerous Bible Studies and devotionals, workshops, online conferences, and training courses (www.flourishwriters.com).

Two of my fellow Flourish writing buddies stepped right up to the plate at the first request for their help. Thanks so much to my Beta Readers, Kelly Hayes, Pennsylvania and Sue Tigro, New Jersey. I have appreciation in my heart for the gifts of time, energy, and effort you gave to me by previewing my manuscript first. Your feedback was crucial to my completion.

Our God calls us to have faith like a Mustard Seed. In Matthew 17:20, we read that we can move mountains with faith this size.

Myrtle Point, Mt. LeConte, Smoky Mountains, Tennessee, June 2016.

Portions from the profits of this book will be given to MUST Ministries Elizabeth Inn Homeless Shelter, The Extension, The Davis Direction Foundation, and The Gideons International.

"Polly Page," the mascot for my blog, *Pages From Joan* is a fun, whimsical character to have around!

Memory Addition

Pages from our Memory Collage Book
Memory Collage Book Back Story

In June 2009, Laura Lea and I in our early fifties decided to create a book to mark this decade. Less than two years earlier, we'd held on as we said, "See you later!" to our mom. The very first image in the book was taken in May 2008. As we took in the spring sunshine on the lake, neither of us could have imagined that the year before us would include such a painful passage of time.

As we began our life-giving project of filling this book, we prayed that the years ahead would be years of healing.

Since we both enjoy collaging, it would include photos, collages, and well, loads of memories. Weddings and new babies would be recognized, among other important events. We would pass the book back and forth between us, completing pages, until all of the pages were full.

The date was Saturday, August 22, 2020. A few of the ladies in our family were gathered together at Tea Leaves and Thyme in Woodstock, Georgia. The special occasion was to shower bride-to-be, CC Cofer who would soon wed my nephew, Kevin Seder in October 2020.

Laura decided to take our Memory Collage Book and read something Mama had written.

Here is what Laura Lea shared that day:

> *Our Family is a circle of*
> *strength and love.*
> *With every birth and every union,*
> *the circle grows stronger.*
> *Every joy shared adds more*
> *love, every crisis faced together*
> *makes the circle stronger.*

As our celebration for CC continued, our nieces passed our Memory Collage Book. Amy, with tears in her eyes said, "Please find a way to share copies of this with all of us!"

While it was impractical to include all eighty completed pages, we selected quite a few to share here.

LOVE

"Beloved, if God so loved us, we also ought to love one another. No one has seen God at any time. If we love one another, God abides in us, and his love has been perfected in us."
1 John 4:11-12

"...and now I will show you the most excellent way."
1 Corinthians 12:31

"By this all will know that you are My disciples, if you have love for one another."
John 13:35

"If there's one thing I hope I showed you, just give love to all."

lyrics taken from a song in the video production by granddaughter, Emily Seder

LauraLea   Joan

Here we are   at LakeHaven in
May, 2008. We are 50 something Women
and we had not a clue that the year
before us would include such a painful
Passage of time. Today is Sunday, June 14,
2009. We pray it will be a year of healing.
    We will share this book back and
forth until every page is filled. We will
"Figure it Out" and move forward, knowing
GOD has prepared the way. L³

June has come Friday, 6/26/09 to pass A year has gone by since Brad's accident. Rhys & I saw Pamela today and it is wonderful to spend time with her.

We are spending the first part of July 2009 up at Lake Haven. I had hoped and prayed that Brad would be well enough to experience the Peachtree Road Race. Instead Rhys and I will be on the boat at Lake Haven on Lake Blue Ridge. Thank you, ¡O + Donny, £₃

"I've dreamt in my life dreams that have changed my ideas; They've gone through me . . . like wine through water, and altered the color of my mind."
—Emily Brontë

SAVING GRACE

real

24/7

The Reverend and Mrs. Evan Shivers

request the honour of your presence

at the marriage of their daughter

Polly

to

Dr. John Wade Walker, junior

on Thursday, the twenty-first of October

at half after seven o'clock

First Baptist Church

Rossville, Georgia

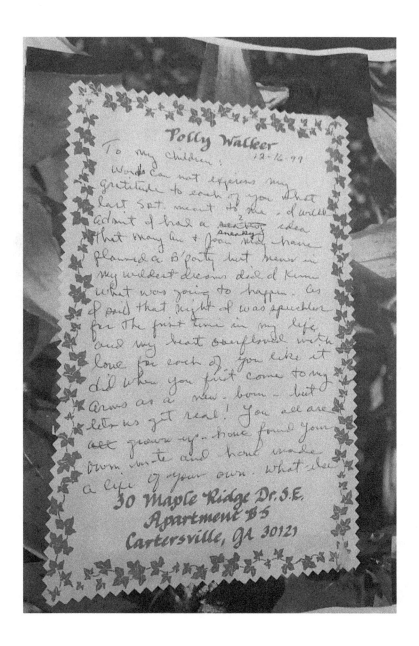

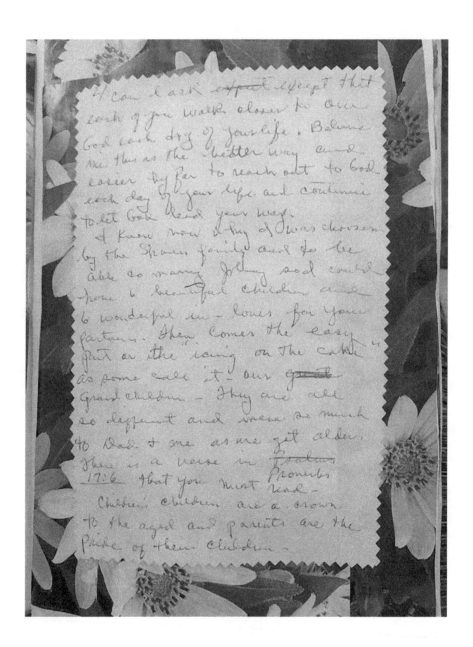

I can l ask expect except that each of you walk closer to Our God each day of your life. Believe me this is the better way and easier by far to reach out to God each day of your life and continue to let God lead your way.

I know now why I was chosen by the Shows family and to be able to marry Johnny and could have 6 beautiful children and 6 wonderful in-laws for your partners. Then comes the easy part or the "icing on the cake" as some call it — our great Grand children — They are all so different and mean so much to Dad & me as we get older. There is a verse in Psalms Proverbs 17:6 that you must read —

Children's children are a crown to the aged and parents are the pride of their children —

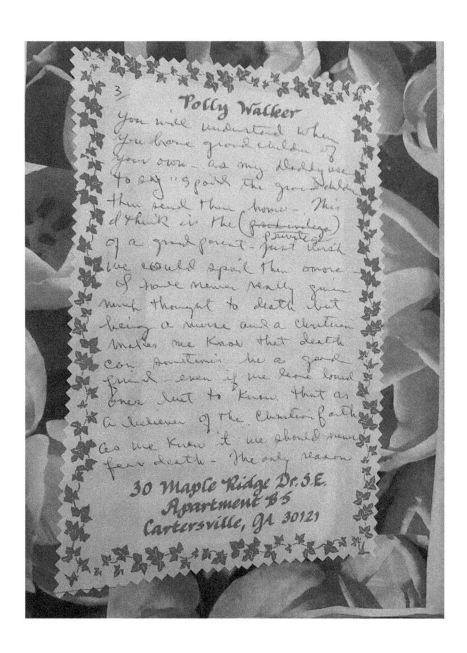

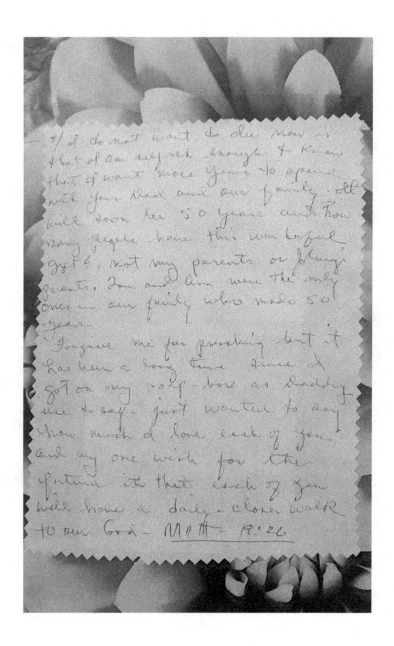

PATIENCE

P is for parental love. Does that mean I love you or you love me?

A is for adoration for all you do.

T is for the Time you give to me and others

I is for the information you share every time I ask.

E is for encouragement. It is my turn to encourage you.

N is for now, today is a gift, the present.

C is for caring and again it is my turn.

E is for each and every moment we are together, here or there.

All my love, Laura Lea, 8-23-06

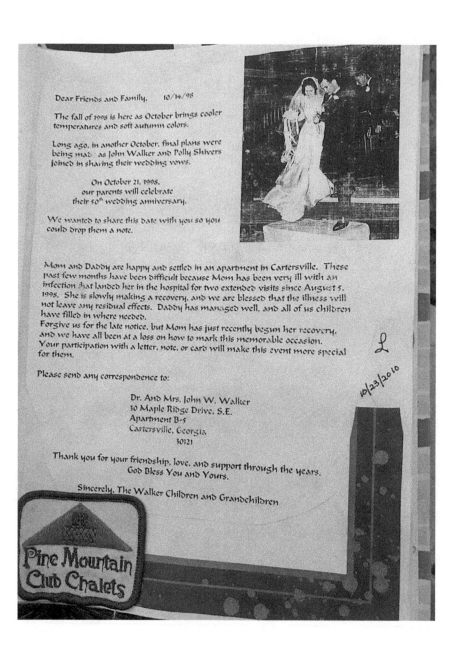

Dear Friends and Family,   10/14/98

The fall of 1998 is here as October brings cooler temperatures and soft autumn colors.

Long ago, in another October, final plans were being made as John Walker and Polly Shivers joined in sharing their wedding vows.

On October 21, 1998, our parents will celebrate their 50th wedding anniversary.

We wanted to share this date with you so you could drop them a note.

Mom and Daddy are happy and settled in an apartment in Cartersville. These past few months have been difficult because Mom has been very ill with an infection that landed her in the hospital for two extended visits since August 5, 1998. She is slowly making a recovery, and we are blessed that the illness will not leave any residual effects. Daddy has managed well, and all of us children have filled in where needed.

Forgive us for the late notice, but Mom has just recently begun her recovery, and we have all been at a loss on how to mark this memorable occasion. Your participation with a letter, note, or card will make this event more special for them.

Please send any correspondence to:

Dr. And Mrs. John W. Walker
30 Maple Ridge Drive, S.E.
Apartment B-5
Cartersville, Georgia
30121

Thank you for your friendship, love, and support through the years. God Bless You and Yours.

Sincerely, The Walker Children and Grandchildren

10/23/2010

314

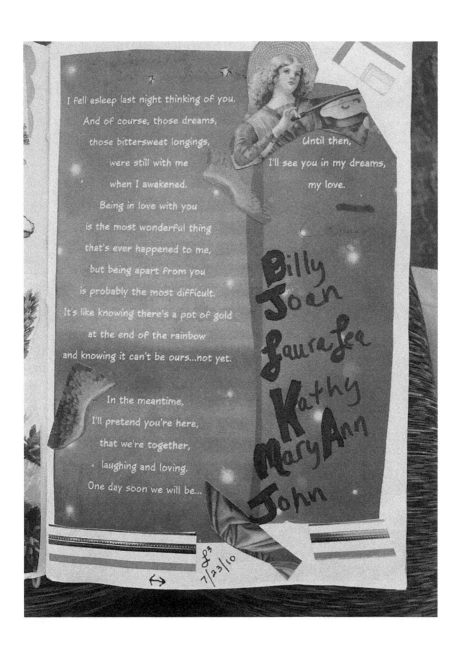

1/19/2013. Our Mom still brings so much color to our lives! L

A Service of Worship and
Celebration

in Memory of

Polly Shivers Walker
December 20, 1927 ~ October 24, 2006

When the perishable has been clothed with the imperishable,
and the mortal with immortality,
then the saying that is written will come true:
"Death has been swallowed up in victory."
"Where, O death, is your victory?
Where, O death, is your sting?"
1 Corinthians 15:54-55 (NIV)

COLORS

Owen Chapel
October 26, 2006
11:00 a.m.

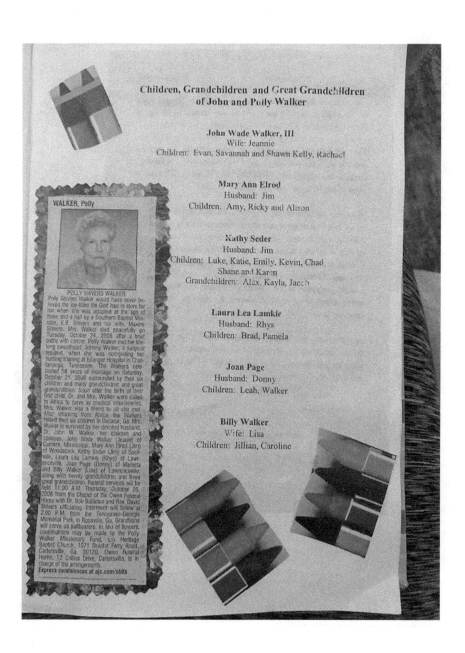

Children, Grandchildren and Great Grandchildren
of John and Polly Walker

John Wade Walker, III
Wife: Jeannie
Children: Evan, Savannah and Shawn Kelly, Rachael

Mary Ann Elrod
Husband: Jim
Children: Amy, Ricky and Alison

Kathy Seder
Husband: Jim
Children: Luke, Katie, Emily, Kevin, Chad, Shane and Karen
Grandchildren: Alex, Kayla, Jacob

Laura Lea Lamkie
Husband: Rhys
Children: Brad, Pamela

Joan Page
Husband: Donny
Children: Leah, Walker

Billy Walker
Wife: Lisa
Children: Jillian, Caroline

WALKER, Polly

POLLY SHIVERS WALKER

Polly Shivers Walker would have never believed the joy-filled life God had in store for her when she was adopted at the age of three and a half by a Southern Baptist Minister, E.B. Shivers and his wife, Maxine Shivers. Mrs. Walker died peacefully on Tuesday, October 24, 2006 after a brief battle with cancer. Polly Walker met her life-long sweetheart, Johnny Walker, a surgical resident, when she was completing her nursing training at Erlanger Hospital in Chattanooga, Tennessee. The Walkers celebrated 58 years of marriage on Saturday, October 21, 2006 surrounded by their six children and many grandchildren and great grandchildren. Soon after the birth of their first child, Dr. and Mrs. Walker were called to Africa to serve as medical missionaries. Mrs. Walker was a friend to all she met. After returning from Africa, the Walkers raised their six children in Decatur, Ga. Mrs. Walker is survived by her devoted husband, Dr. John W. Walker, her children and spouses, John Wade Walker (Jeanie) of Carriere, Mississippi, Mary Ann Elrod (Jim) of Woodstock, Kathy Seder (Jim) of Snellville, Laura Lea Lamkie (Rhys) of Lawrenceville, Joan Page (Donny) of Marietta and Billy Walker (Lisa) of Lawrenceville, along with twenty grandchildren, and three great grandchildren. Funeral services will be held 11:00 A.M. Thursday, October 26, 2006 from the Chapel of the Owen Funeral Home with Dr. Bob Ballance and Rev. David Shivers officiating. Interment will follow at 2:00 P.M. from the Tennessee-Georgia Memorial Park, in Rossville, Ga. Grandsons will serve as pallbearers. In lieu of flowers, contributions may be made to the Polly Walker Missionary Fund, c/o Heritage Baptist Church, 1071 Douthit Ferry Road, Cartersville, Ga. 30120. Owen Funeral Home, 12 Collins Drive, Cartersville, is in charge of the arrangements.
Express condolences at ajc.com/obits

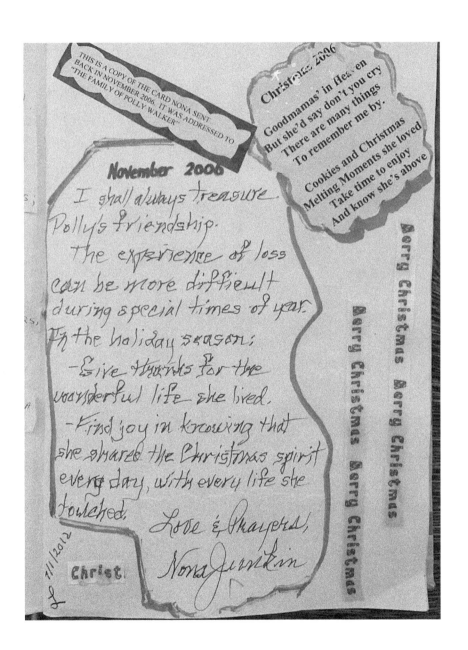

THIS IS A COPY OF THE CARD NONA SENT BACK IN NOVEMBER 2006. IT WAS ADDRESSED TO "THE FAMILY OF POLLY WALKER"

Christmas 2006

Goodmamas' in Heaven
But she'd say don't you cry
There are many things
To remember me by.

Cookies and Christmas
Melting Moments she loved
Take time to enjoy
And know she's above

November 2006

I shall always treasure Polly's friendship.

The experience of loss can be more difficult during special times of year. In the holiday season:

- Give thanks for the wonderful life she lived.
- Find joy in knowing that she shared the Christmas spirit every day, with every life she touched.

Love & Prayers,
Nona Junikin

Merry Christmas Merry Christmas

Merry Christmas Merry Christmas

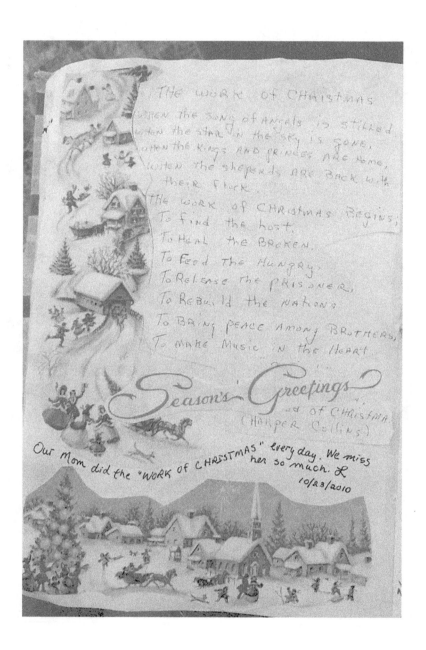

THE WORK OF CHRISTMAS

WHEN the song of Angels is stilled,
when the star in the sky is gone,
when the Kings AND princes Are home,
When the shepers Are Back with
their flock.
THE WORK OF CHRISTMAS Begins;
To find the host,
To Heal the Broken,
To Feed The Hungry,
To Release the prisoner,
To Rebuild the nations
To Bring peace Among Brothers,
To make Music in the Heart

Season's Greetings

...d of CHRISTMAS
(HARPER Collins)

Our Mom did the "WORK OF CHRISTMAS" every day. We miss her so much. L
10/23/2010

Our Mom loved books and was always reading and writing notes. Since her death, 10-24-2006, her prayers and thoughts linger with us as we reread her Bibles and books. Even though she is gone, this entry from "My Utmost for HIS HIGHEST", proves she has been thinking and praying for each one of us for all our lives. Her note was written 10 years ago and her love for us has never changed. She knew we would face tough, uncertain times. So as you read, let's take this advice to heart and

"Let's Roll".

Share with children 1999

What To Do Under The Conditions   April 13th

- *"Cast your cares on the Lord."* PSALM 55:22.

We must distinguish between the burden-bearing that is right and the burden-bearing that is wrong. We ought never to bear the burden of sin or of doubt, but there are burdens placed on us by God which He does not intend to lift off, He wants us to roll them back on Him. "Cast that he hath given thee upon the Lord." (R.V. marg.) If we undertake work for God and get out of touch with Him, the sense of responsibility will be overwhelmingly crushing; but if we roll back on God that which He has put upon us, He takes away the sense of responsibility by bringing in the realization of Himself.

Many workers have gone out with high courage and fine impulses, but with no intimate fellowship with Jesus Christ, and before long they are crushed. They do not know what to do with the burden, it produces weariness, and people say—"What an embittered end to such a beginning!"

"Roll thy burden upon the Lord"—you have been bearing it all; deliberately put one end on the shoulders of God. "The government will be on his shoulders." Commit to God "that he hath given thee"; not fling it off, but put it over on to Him and yourself with it, and the burden is lightened by the sense of companionship. Never disassociate yourself from the burden.

2/21/09 £3

Sandy Springs Baptist Church

F 8/16/2014

Desiderata

Go placidly amid the noise and haste, and remember what peace there may be in silence.

As far as possible without surrender be on good terms with all persons.

Speak your truth quietly and clearly; and listen to others, even the dull and ignorant; they too have their story.

Avoid loud and aggressive persons, they are vexations to the spirit.

If you compare yourself with others, you may become vain and bitter; for always there will be greater and lesser persons than yourself.

Enjoy your achievements as well as your plans.

Keep interested in your career, however humble; it is a real possession in the changing fortunes of time.

Exercise caution in your business affairs; for the world is full of trickery.

But let this not blind you to what virtue there is; many persons strive for high ideals; and everywhere life is full of heroism.

Be yourself.

Especially, do not feign affection.

Neither be critical about love; for in the face of all aridity and disenchantment it is as perennial as the grass.

Take kindly the counsel of the years, gracefully surrendering the things of youth.

Nurture strength of spirit to shield you in sudden misfortune. But do not distress yourself with imaginings.

Many fears are born of fatigue and loneliness. Beyond a wholesome discipline, be gentle with yourself.

You are a child of the universe, no less than the trees and the stars; you have a right to be here.

And whether or not it is clear to you, no doubt the universe is unfolding as it should.

Therefore be at peace with God, whatever you conceive Him to be, and whatever your labors and aspirations, in the noisy confusion of life keep peace with your soul.

With all its sham, drudgery and broken dreams, it is still a beautiful world. Be careful. Strive to be happy.

© Max Ehrmann 1927

This poem was framed in our parents bedroom as we were growing up. Read j's October 2014 blog. "Fifty something Women". 11/2/2014 L.

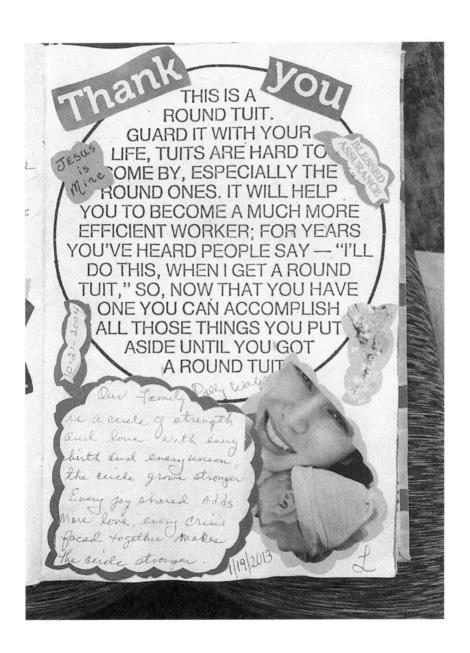

time." Moms must provide the necessary companionship, instruction, and moral incentive by demonstrating in their personal behavior what truth, goodness, and loving concern for others.

...ean.

...ert Louis Stevenson explained it convincingly in these words: "To be rich in admiration and free from envy; to rejoice greatly in the good of others, to love with such generosity of heart that your love is still a dear possession in absence or unkindness, these are gifts which money cannot buy, and in many cases, which only a wise and devoted mother can bestow as the greatest of all possessions to her children."

hardship and suffering. But in every generation, children who receive adequate amounts of love, advice and personal attention usually grow up to become competent, reliable citizens. Today,

however, in many America), spend hours alone, unsupervise... role moms play in shaping our destiny: "God could not be everywhere at one time, so He invented mothers."

us be grateful to make happy.
the charming gardeners who
make our souls blossom.

Joan W. Page

Dr. John WALKER
Dr. Walker → MOTHERS
DAuGHTers
MARy AnN   770-241-9966
JOAN- 404-281-3255
Kathy 404 519-0908
LauraLea 678-910-1749
GLC 10/22 ———11/29/2013.

111 TOWER ROAD • MARIETTA, GA 30060 • (770) 421-7400
...berton Place is affiliated with the WellStar Health System

1/19/2013

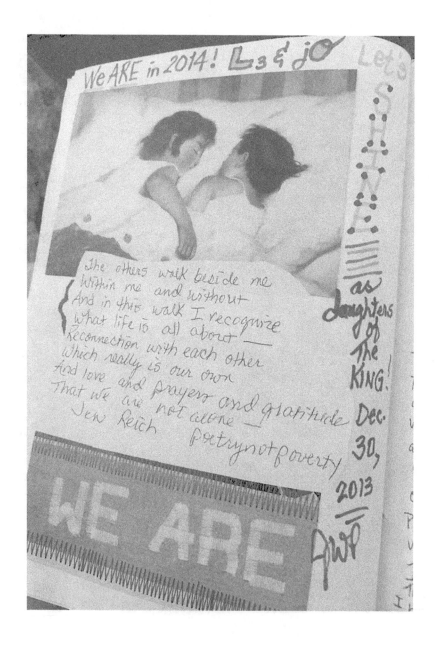

Mama and her six girls, Lisa, Joan, Jeanie, Laura, Mary Ann and Kathy. August 16, 1986. We gathered at a reception at The Lamkie Home to send Mama and Daddy back to Africa as missionaries, once again.

Polly and her Johnny celebrating wedding number six:
Billy and Lisa Walker, November 21, 1987.

NOTATIONS

NOTATIONS

NOTATIONS

NOTATIONS

NOTATIONS

NOTATIONS

NOTATIONS

NOTATIONS

About the Author

Joan Walker Page was blessed to be the daughter of the main character in these stories, Polly Shivers Walker. Forever wouldn't be enough time to reap all of the benefits of having this wise woman for a mother. However, the wonderful forty-seven years they shared certainly made a significant impression on Joan's life. Joan is a blogger and first-time author, and she holds a bachelor's degree from The University of Georgia and a master's degree from Georgia State University. She spent many years as an educator in the Atlanta area. She enjoys time with her growing family, girlfriends, adventures, and worthy causes. Joan, her husband, Donny, and their toy goldendoodle, Camden "Cami" divide their time between Marietta, Georgia, and Lake Blue Ridge in the North Georgia Mountains.